Contents

Dedicated to the memory of my father Granville,
my wife Sarah, and my mother Frances.
All three left this earth a better place and while
here touched me as no others did or will.
Mahalo

Library of Congress Catalog Card Number: 96-92056

First Printing 1996

10 9 8 7 6 5 4 3 2 1

Printed in the United States of America

SUCCESS MADE EASY

RON MARTIN

SUCCESS
DYNAMICS

Foreword

by Wyland

The world's greatest ocean artist

When I met Ron Martin, Wyland Galleries Hawaii had sales of $1 million a year. A few years later, our sales were more than $20 million a year.

My partner Bill and I are grateful to Ron for making our success easy. It really is easy when you know how. In **Success Made Easy,** Ron shares his unique insight that re-shapes the way each of us thinks about our own success.

Ron's easy formulas have taken our company and staff through what most people called recessionary times. We talked with Ron one day, took a vote, and decided not to participate in the recession.

Instead, we followed Ron's strategic program of **Success Made Easy**. It was that simple. This fantastic book provides an easy-to-follow road map to help us ful-fill our dreams.

I truly believe if you read this great book you will be taking your first big step on the road to success and happiness.

Best Fishes...

Wyland

Chapter 1

Believe Success

"Discovering success is like opening a safe.
Once you know the combination, It's Easy..."

Everyone can have success. **It's Easy.**

Success is more than money. Success is happiness, satisfaction, health and wealth.

Success begins with belief. **Think and Grow Rich** author Napoleon Hill said, "Whatever the mind can conceive and *believe*, it can achieve."

Look in the mirror. You are God's human creation. You were created to succeed.

What others have done, you can do as well.

"We hold these truths to be self-evident
that all men are created equal..."
THOMAS JEFFERSON

Those words were first written in the Declaration of Independence in 1776. I first heard them in church in

1952. I was a teenage, Episcopalian altar boy and wanted to believe the church, but I wasn't one for unconditional belief without some evidence.

The evidence against equality was stacked pretty high in my mind. I was in junior high school, and any physical education class made it clear that all of us boys were not "equal." If we were *created equal,* why are we so different?

Some boys could run like the wind, others were blown backwards by it. Some were as tall as oak trees, others half as big, yet the same age. *What's the deal here?*

Some were good at football and baseball, others good at basketball and volleyball. Some ran track, while others ran for school office. I joined the band, but not without trying everything else.

I sat on the sidelines and played my snare drum while the athletes played on the field. In some ways I felt cheated. Why didn't I have the long legs and big muscles? I wondered what Thomas Jefferson really meant when he said *"equal."*

I attended a lower middle-class, all-white school in Southern California. One day we church altar boys took a field trip and visited fellow altar boys in an all-black neighborhood called Watts.

None of us had ever been to Watts. The altar boys in Watts looked different from us. They talked differently and lived differently. They wore old, worn, hand-me-down clothes. We were wearing our "Sunday best." The street was their playground. We had beautiful public parks.

They stood on one side of the street; we stood on the other. We looked across the street at each other not quite knowing what to do or say. The adults threw us together after church and told us to go outside and play.

The buildings were run-down, and trash littered the street. I kept wondering if all men really were created equal. This didn't look fair to me. My exposure to this different reality left a lasting impression.

I wondered if Thomas Jefferson understood the human condition in 1776. Obviously not; it was 90 years after he wrote about equality that the Fifteenth Amendment of the Constitution gave black men the right to vote.

Women, of any color, did not get to vote in the United States until the Nineteenth Amendment in 1920. I wondered, "How were we equal?" I scratched my head with this question for another 15 years or so.

I finished high school, went in and out of the Air Force, had a few jobs, started a business of my own and took an interest in self help books, especially Napoleon Hill's **Think & Grow Rich**, and W. Clement Stone's **Success Through A Positive Mental Attitude**.

I first met W. Clement Stone through his writings, then later in person. Stone is a successful businessman, philanthropist and author. He says that human beings have a brain and nervous system unequaled by any computer.

 I began to think that maybe this is one way we are all equal. We all have a brain and nervous system that allow us to think, plan and feel our way to success. It's easy.

If so, then why isn't everyone living in mansions, driving luxury cars, dining in the finest restaurants and traveling leisurely around the world? Something is missing.

Another area of equality is time. We all get the same amount of time, but it sure doesn't seem like it. Some people do more than others. *What's the deal here?*

People say, "There isn't enough time in the day," or "I don't have time to do it," or "I ran out of time," or "I don't have time to exercise, to read or to think."

Time is precious, isn't it? Consider this: if you work eight hours a day, seven days a week, and sleep eight hours every night, you still have eight hours a day, or 56 hours a week not working or sleeping.

If you work 40 hours a week, you have 72 hours of non-sleeping, non-working time. Your future is determined by how you spend your "available time."

 You were "created equal." You were born with a human brain and nervous system, and given 24 hours a day to use it.

Your physical makeup, heredity, birthplace or ancestors do not govern your success.

The world is full of educated failures and ignorant successes.

Chapter 2

Think Success

"Success is easy when you take control of your thoughts."

Imagine this... someone gives you an audio cassette tape. The tape is a recording of your own thoughts for the last 24 hours.

Along with the tape comes an assignment. You must listen to the tape and list all of your thoughts in one of two categories. In one category list your positive and constructive thoughts. In the other your negative and destructive thoughts.

Which list would be longer?

Your mind is always turned on. There is no "pause" or "off" switch. When you listen to your imaginary tape on your man-made tape player, you can pause it or turn it off and think.

The thoughts on the tape never stop. There are no blank spaces. You think when you are awake; you think when you are asleep.

If your positive/constructive thoughts (in 24 hours) were stacked on one side of a scale, and your negative/destructive thoughts on the other, which way would the scale tip?

 You decide what you think about.
What you think about, you bring about.

Hawaii is unique. Millionaires and homeless people live in the same neighborhoods, walk the same streets and go to the same beaches.

The rich and the poor mingle, and when in swimsuits, cannot be told apart. They sit together on Waikiki Beach and gaze at rainbows, sunrises and sunsets. They daydream as they watch surfers, sailboats and sunbathers, and it's all free. They are both enjoying **success**.

I've had conversations with the penthouse dwellers as well as the "stairway dwellers." There are some very intelligent people living with very little, using their "street smarts" to get by. They reach their goals. **They are successful**.

The difference between these two success groups is their goals. They want different things. Both are okay. Both are successful. Which group would you prefer to be a part of?

You are surrounded by the things you want, *badly enough.*

At my success rallies I ask people: "Have you ever bought anything you couldn't afford?" I always get a big laugh when everyone's hand goes up in the air. Buying something you can't afford is a great example of mind over matter. Everyone does it. **It's easy.**

To exercise mind over matter, control your conscious thoughts until your subconscious is focused on what you really want.

What is meant by *conscious/subconscious*?

Imagine holding a grain of sand between your thumb and forefinger. Let that grain of sand represent the power and size of your *conscious* mind.

Now imagine your *subconscious* mind as being all of the sand on all the beaches in the world.

Have you heard the story about a woman lifting her car to free her trapped child? There are many documented examples of human beings doing superhuman feats in a time of extreme emotion. Such events are the result of someone's subconscious taking control and satisfying a dominant need.

You can attract that same power and create a flow of energy running through you that will guarantee your success.

Achieving any level of success you want is easier than picking up a car. Just make success your dominant thought. Get emotional about your success. Get your subconscious involved.

It's easy.

In sports some athletes function at a "superhuman" level. Everyone wonders how they do it. Many great basketball players played the game before Michael Jordan. What makes him stand out in an all-star crowd and be called the best ever? If you could "listen in" on Michael's mind tape for 24 hours, you would see how he makes it look so **easy**.

Your dominant thoughts attract your subconscious powers. When listening to your own mind tape, what thought is dominant? What one idea, problem, challenge, concern or vision gets more thought time than any other? Identify it.

 Whatever you think about most, your subconscious believes you want. Eventually, when deemed "a must," it is delivered.

The delivery may come when you least expect it. But, it will come so long as your thought, vision and desire all remain dominant. Your subconscious responds more to feelings and emotions than to logic and words.

You attract the attention of your subconscious whenever you vividly imagine something.

Some people vividly imagine failure. They daydream about not being able to make their car or house payments. They imagine difficulty buying food, and living a life without luxury. Their subconscious is attracted to the strong visions of failure or poverty. You can't paint success pictures in your mind while fearing failure.

 See success, then make that vision dominant on your 24-hour mind tape. It's easy.

A single thought repeated over and over works on your subconscious much like ancient Chinese water torture worked on prisoners. The captors focused drops of water on the center of their prisoners' foreheads until they talked. Eventually, they all talked.

When Cassius Clay became a professional boxer, he immediately told the world two things. First, *"I am The Greatest,"* and second, *"I have such a pretty face."*

Think about his self-bestowed title, "The Greatest." This young boxer could not imagine himself as the "biggest," or the "meanest" or even the "fastest." He knew he wasn't. Cassius Clay didn't need to be the biggest, meanest and fastest. He was "The Greatest."

He announced his "Greatness" prematurely, and angered the macho boxing community. They said: "This kid's body can't back up his big mouth." And, "He can say good-bye to his pretty face! Pretty faces and boxing don't belong together."

The world turned out to see the current champion, the biggest and the meanest, Mr. Sonny Liston, shut this kid up.

After a few rounds with "The Greatest," the *champ* sat on his stool and became a *chump*. Cassius Clay, later known as Muhammed Ali, "The Greatest," maintained his "pretty face" throughout his brilliant boxing career. His subconscious protected his "pretty face."

Muhammed Ali recited his positive thoughts as poetry to accentuate the message to his subconscious. He declared, "I float like a butterfly, I sting like a bee."

Even the biggest, meanest and fastest can't hit a butterfly, and they would all feel the sting from a tiny bee.

What were Sonny Liston's thoughts as the young Muhammed Ali danced in front of him, taunting him to get off his stool? What was the defeated champ's dominant thought at that moment? It might have been: "I wish I was dead."

He might have felt the same way the next morning when the press came to interview him. That thought may have become dominant and seeped through to his subconscious. Maybe it was reluctantly accepted, and delivered. Sonny Liston was found face-down in his swimming pool a few years later.

Your will to live is dominant. Your subconscious controls thousands of bodily functions every day without a conscious thought.

For example, take breathing. To test the relative power of your conscious versus subconscious, just hold your breath. In a moment or so, your subconscious will begin to *talk* to you. It will say "Okay, enough! Take a breath." But if your conscious power is strong enough, you may hold your breath for two or three minutes before your subconscious *screams* at you.

If you refuse to breathe, your subconscious will simply render your conscious unconscious. Your subconscious will take control and start breathing for you.

You cannot commit suicide by holding your breath. Parents of some willful young children discover this fact when they watch their defiant child turn blue, pass out and then resume breathing.

Can you hold your eyelids open for a day, or not eat for a month? Your subconscious saves your life during emergencies, and maintains your basic bodily functions daily. It can also **make your success easy**.

 Decide what you want, then develop a burning desire to achieve it. Build a "fire of desire."

You create a burning desire by consciously imagining your desired result until it becomes your dominant thought. Displace any thoughts of *fear* or *failure* with thoughts of *hope* and *success.*

Your 24-hour personal mind tape is always full. To change the thought mixture, force in positive/constructive thoughts. Negative/destructive thoughts will be forced out. This process is called displacement. One thought takes the place of another.

Imagine your 24 hours of thinking as a full bucket of water. If you were to throw handfuls of sand into a full bucket of water, eventually the sand would displace all of the water. You can turn a bucket of water into a bucket of sand without dumping out the water.

You can turn a negative attitude into a positive attitude the same way. You can feed thoughts and images of your goals into your mind, and displace thoughts and images of your doubts and fears. **You can make success your dominant thought.**

Be aware of what you are thinking, then control it.

 Your paradigms are beliefs that control the way you think and act. A paradigm is like the frame around a painting. Your success is framed by your beliefs.

Ask a group of people, "What's a schoolteacher?" Everyone will have a different "paradigm," depending on their personal experiences. Someone who attended Catholic school will think of a school teacher quite differently than someone who attended an inner-city public school.

Your self-paradigms control you. Your experiences might make success hard to believe. If there is something you want, but don't have, you may wonder: "Why don't I have it?"

Your mind will answer the questions you ask through its established paradigms.

The answer might be: "Because you don't deserve it," or "You can't afford it" or "You're not smart enough" or "You don't have the education." The problem is not the answer, the problem is the question.

The success or failure of your early role models helped to create your paradigms. My father struggled his entire life to keep his head above water. My uncles and aunts all worked hard, but lived on the financial edge. My parents' success determined where I lived, and in that neighborhood I met children with lives much like mine.

We all lived in similar houses, had similar cars and engaged in activities we could afford. That was all I knew. I thought everyone in the world was just like us, struggling to get by. I believed that I would grow up to struggle, just like my father and everyone around me.

Television came into our house when I was a pre-teen. This new toy gave me a glimpse of lives much different from mine.

My family paradigms began to shift as I watched programs like "Ozzie and Harriet." "Do people really live like that?" I wondered. Harriet existed for her husband Ozzie, and her sons, David and Ricky.

They had daily adventures unlike anyone I knew. Their family didn't have to struggle for nice things like mine did.

Ozzie was always home reading, or playing basketball with David and Ricky while Harriet prepared the family dinner. There was a feeling of love, harmony and, most noticeably to me, security. Did Ozzie have a job? How did they pay the mortgage on their beautiful suburban home? I wondered, *"What's the deal here?"*

My dad worked seven days a week. He came home late and tired. He ate dinner in the kitchen with my mother, then drank his Early Times whiskey until he passed out.

I wondered: "What's normal, my life or 'Ozzie and Harriet'?" I started to believe my life could be better than it was.

There's a story about a farmer's son who climbed a cliff and discovered an eagle's nest. The young boy took an eagle's egg home and put it under one of his chickens. The chicken hatched and cared for the baby eagle.

As the young eagle looked around, he saw only chickens. He saw himself as just another chicken. He plucked around the barnyard eating chicken feed. He had no idea how different he was from the chickens.

There was no roof over the barnyard; the chickens didn't try to fly. They were content to pluck around.

The eagle grew huge wings, but never tried to fly. One day an adult eagle flew low over the chicken coop. The chickens ran for cover; the young eagle looked in amazement.

Inspired, he ran around the barn-yard, flapping his large, unused wings. Soon he was airborne, and he flew off towards the mountains. He never looked back, and never returned to the barnyard. This young eagle had a major, instant paradigm shift. He "flew the coop."

I'll always remember my first drive through Beverly Hills. I kept thinking, "Do people really live here? How do they afford it?"

 I thought: "If they can do it, I can do it."

W. Clement Stone observed that successful people use R^2A^2. They *Recognize, Relate, Assimilate* and *Apply*. They learn and grow by paying attention to what's going on around them. When they read, study or experience life, they practice R^2A^2. So can you.

First, *recognize* what law or principle is being demonstrated. Next, *relate* that wisdom back to your own life or situation, then *assimilate* it. Absorb it, make it your own.

Next *apply* it. Make it a part of your life from now on. R^2A^2 allows you to make instant paradigm shifts to better your life.

Say for example, you hear about a celebrity dying of lung cancer. As you *recognize* what happened, you discover that the celebrity was a smoker. When you *relate* this experience to your life, you know that you also smoke.

You *assimilate* this new knowledge, think about it and decide that you do not want to die of lung cancer.

You *apply* what you just learned, quit smoking and save your life. **Easy**.

R^2A^2 allows you to learn and grow from the experiences of others.

You don't have to suffer from lung cancer to quit smoking. You don't have to endure years of struggle to discover success.

Chapter 3

See Success

I keep six honest serving men.
Their names are What and Why and When
and How and Where and Who..."
KIPLING, *THE SERVING MEN*

Computer programmers say: "GIGO." Garbage In, Garbage Out. Feed bad information into a computer, and bad information will come out. Computers store information, then retrieve it on demand in a variety of ways.

Businesses input revenue figures that allow them to plan, budget and expect results. Computers help businesses eliminate surprises. As the data bank in the computer expands, the accuracy of the predictions increases. Top executives with million-dollar salaries look at "the numbers" and strategize their success.

The validity of "the numbers" depends upon accurate data input. A data input typist can make a small mistake that renders "the numbers" meaningless.

The million-dollar executive can steer the company ship onto the rocks while thinking it is headed out to the high seas.

Your mind works much the same way. You store daily thoughts and beliefs into your mental data bank for future use. Your "data entry department" works 24 hours a day, storing your every thought.

You generate the thoughts, either intentionally or unintentionally. Someone might say something to you that triggers certain thoughts. You store these thoughts instantly as you continue to think new ones.

The words to a song might trigger a memory. Thoughts might be triggered by a sign on the road or a face in a crowd. "Thought triggers" are everywhere.

People go to church to think about God. The "thought triggers" inside the church make it **easy**.

 Ambush yourself with "thought triggers" that cause you to think about your goals. Control your mind.

Much has been written about how people control other people. Studies reveal how eye contact, facial expressions, voice modulation and body language control people.

The best way to control thinking is to ask questions. Questions demand answers, and answers require thought. When someone asks you a question, your mind instantaneously scrolls through every thought you have ever had on the subject to come up with the answer.

 Lawyers control witnesses with questions. Teachers control students with questions. You can control yourself with questions.

Your thoughts might be a million miles away when you are asked a question. Your mind instantly changes directions and answers the question.

As you listen to your 24-hour mind tape, you will hear yourself asking and answering general questions like:

"What time is it?"
"What am I going to eat for dinner tonight?"
"What will I do this weekend?"

You might also hear negative questions like:

"Can I pay my rent?"
"Can I make my car payment?"
"Why can't I succeed?"

Instead, ask yourself positive questions like:

"How, when and where can I succeed?"

**When you intentionally ask yourself
the right questions, you take control.**

The lesson above changed my life in one day. The year was 1967. I had recently broken out of *prison*. Let me clarify that. I had recently quit my job and started my own business.

Becoming independent is a wonderful feeling. I soon discovered that my new boss (me) was the most understanding boss I could have.

I got up in the morning and asked myself a question, "What am I going to do today?" Working for someone else, I didn't get to ask myself that question. I already knew the answer or I asked my boss.

Whenever I asked my old boss what he wanted me to do today, he always had a quick answer. His data bank was full of things he wanted done.

As I asked myself (my new boss) this same question, different options were offered. My new boss responded with, "Well, you could go to your office. Hmmm, or you could play golf, go to the beach or go waterskiing." Which option would you pick?

Some days I answered myself with, "You have an appointment at your office at 10 a.m., so go in early and get a jump on the day." I would think, "Okay," and do so.

Other days I answered, "You don't have any appoint-ments at the office, so go waterskiing or play golf."

As my recreational skills improved, my business struggled. I slipped deeply into debt. My company ship was heading straight for the rocks. I imagined the wide open horizon, then **boom.**

The phone woke me up at 11 a.m. That should have been a clue that I was off course. Anyone who needs a wake-up call at 11 a.m. after a full night's sleep needs help.

 My wake-up call came from Marvin K. Brown Cadillac in San Diego, California. It went like this: "Mr. Martin, we want your Cadillac back." I woke up!

My first exposure to a Cadillac was 10 years earlier. "Cadillac" meant more to me than just a fancy car. I was 14 years old and my grandfather came to visit in his brand-new, white 1956 Cadillac Limousine. I sat in the car, played with the electric windows and imagined owning a Cadillac someday. I liked the feeling.

Grandfather had "struck it rich." He discovered a uranium mine somewhere in the desert. They carried the uranium ore out by the carloads, and the money poured in. Unfortunately the uranium vein ran out, and so did the money. Granddaddy lost his Caddy. He lost everything.

Buying my Cadillac was no small feat. I hadn't struck it rich yet. I wanted to keep the car, badly. My subconscious took over. Here's why.

My Cadillac payments were about $200 per month, and I was five payments behind. I was also four months delinquent on my house payments. I had a wallet full of abused credit cards, and I was running out of grocery stores where I could cash a check.

I had a desk drawer at home reserved for the "mail with the little windows" – the dreaded bill drawer. The envelopes were unopened.

I ducked process servers camping outside my house. I locked my Cadillac in the garage at night, blocked the driveway with my boat, then chained and locked the boat. No one was going to get *my* Cadillac.

I had been asking myself a tough question: "How can I keep this Cadillac without making the payments?"

Now the question was changing. My goal changed. Now I had to keep the Cadillac, **legitimately!** My subconscious spoke through me. I said, "I want to order a new Cadillac." I was driving a 1965; it was now late 1967, and the new 1968's were just coming out.

My proposal was this: "It will take six weeks for my new car to arrive from Detroit. By then I will pay you the $1,000 I owe you, plus the down payment for my new 1968." Silence.

Finally he agreed. Whew! Our conversation changed to the model, color and features of my new Cadillac. In my mind, I was already driving my new car.

I hung up the phone and sat on the edge of the bed. I was wringing wet. I felt like Muhammed Ali defeating Sonny Liston. I was drained. I had won. Yeah!

Then I thought, "Had I won? Had I saved the car?" I asked myself, "How am I going to come up with $1,000?" My inner-self did not suggest waterskiing or golf. I told myself to get up, get dressed and go to my office.

That's all the direction I needed. I flew into action. Soon I was in my office, seated behind my desk.

I started asking myself, "Where can I find $1,000?" The first answer I got was: "Get this place cleaned up!" I didn't know how that was going to get me the money, but I followed instructions anyway. It was a start.

I kept asking myself, "Where can I find $1,000?" I wasn't getting the answer. I changed the question a few times. Eventually, I asked the right question:

 "What can I do right now, this minute, to improve my business?"

This change in wording put a totally different program in my mind. I was no longer looking for money I didn't know how to get. I was now looking for something to *do*. I was now asking a question that I could answer. An answer came quickly. I took action. **It was easy.**

I decided to telephone someone I had neglected calling for a long time. I knew this person wanted to do business with me, but I never thought about her while waterskiing. I called. We did business. She said she was glad that I called. So was I.

I gave a lot of thought to that phone call. I had just "created" money. How did I do it? Who was responsible? Answer: Marvin K. Brown. Without that wake-up call at 11 a.m. I would have slept until noon, then spent an hour deciding what to do that day. I probably would have gone to the golf course because it was too late to go waterskiing. I surely wouldn't have made that phone call.

 My first success took only two minutes after asking the right question.

When I realized the power of my new question, I asked it again:

> *"What can I do right now, this minute, to improve my business?"*

Another "opportunity" came to mind. I took another action. I "created" more money. **It was easy.**

By the end of that day, I was a new man. I had a plan. I knew how I was going to get the money to keep the Cadillac. I was going to "create" it.

The next day, I boldly wrote my newly found *trigger question* on cardstock and plastered it all over my office.

Every word in the question was vital. If I omitted the words "right now, this minute," I would think of things to do next week, next month or next year. I had only six weeks! If I left out "to improve my business," answers like golf or waterskiing came to mind. I needed $1,000!

Behavior determines success. My behavior was changing. I kept asking that question; I still do. Answers kept coming; they still do.

I sat at my desk every night and faced reality. I searched for a bill small enough to match the money I "created," and paid it. I continued the process. I felt good. Feelings follow action.

I got my new Cadillac, kept my house and emptied the "dreaded bill drawer." I've owned 15 new Cadillacs since then. They are symbolic to me.

To this day, I have not had a bill I couldn't pay, or a reality I couldn't face. I operate a very successful business and still find the time to surf and play. All because of one question. If I can ask it, then you can ask it too. Ask yourself:

> **"What can I do right now, this minute,**
> **to create more success?"**

Chapter 4

Program Success

"There is nothing capricious in nature, and the implanting of a desire indicates that its gratification is within the constitution of the creature that feels it..."

EMERSON

Computers are sold with basic programs that allow the user to perform general functions. More sophisticated and specific programs can be purchased at computer stores. You can also write your own programs to perform specific and unique functions.

"Human" computers come with instinctive programs for survival. From the moment of birth, babies develop programs to satisfy their needs. They store information about what's going on around them. They observe who feeds and loves them. They quickly learn how to get what they want.

As an adult, you can develop positive programs that inspire and motivate you to get what you want, or negative programs that excuse you for not getting what you want. It's your choice. **It's easy.**

Listen to your mind tape. Displace any negative programs with *questions* that trigger positive thoughts and actions.

Let's explore a few popular programs people use. See if any of them sound familiar.

POSITIVE/SUCCESS PROGRAM:
"How can I afford it?"
NEGATIVE/FAILURE PROGRAM:
"I can't afford it."

Imagine that you're walking by a new car showroom and you see a car you like. You think, "What a beauty! I sure would like to have that car." Your next thought is a question: "Can I have it?" If the answer is, "No, I can't afford it," your thinking stops right there. You walk away. You don't ask the price. You know you can't afford it, so why ask?

 Emerson said, "There is nothing capricious in nature, and the implanting of a desire indicates that its gratification is within the constitution of the creature that feels it."

Think about Emerson's words. I first heard that quote on an audio tape in 1968. I rewound the tape and played it again and again. I sensed something important was being said, but I was not accustomed to Emerson's style of writing.

I wrote the statement down and analyzed his words. Simply put, Emerson is saying that there are no surprises and you would not *want* something if you could not *have* it.

Penniless people sitting on the curb thinking about a bottle of wine do not *want* the fancy cars driving by. They do, however, *want* and *get* their next bottle of wine.

Begging for money is the toughest job in the world. Think of the rejection, disappointment, abuse and disrespect these people must overcome. They stay focused on their goal. They get what they want. **They succeed.**

 What you make dominant in your mind will eventually manifest itself.

How can you make that car in the showroom yours? When you hear yourself saying, "I *can't* afford it," displace the "*can't* word" with a dominating and controlling *question.*

Be careful how you phrase the question. A question like "Why *can't* I afford it?" might get you an answer you *don't want* to hear.

"I can't," results in: "So why try?" If you can't afford it, then why even think about it? Right? **Wrong!**

Remember Emerson's message: You wouldn't *want* it if you couldn't *have* it. You will figure out how to get it if you *want* it *badly enough.*

Now, ask yourself the right question: "What *can* I do to afford that car?" Keep asking the question. Your subconscious knows the answer.

Displace the word *"can't"* with the question, *"How?"*

You can have that car, or house, or business, or job, or vacation, or relationship or anything else you want. Keep asking yourself, "How?" The answer will come. It may come when you least expect it.

POSITIVE/SUCCESS PROGRAM:
"How can I get more organized?"
NEGATIVE/FAILURE PROGRAM:
"I can't get organized."

Organization is vital. Without organization you have chaos. I've had different levels of organization imposed upon me at different times in my life. First it was mom conditioning me to brush my teeth and clean my room.

As I went from parental influences to those of roommates, I experienced disorganization and chaos. At one time, my life was so unorganized that finding a spoon or fork meant rummaging through the kitchen drawers searching for one.

At another time, the rule was: "Everything has a home, and that's where it lives."

Organizing little details and tasks improves your entire day. Without organization, you might procrastinate as you decide what to do next. Result: Time spent doing nothing.

I've attended seminars that taught us how to use file folders and drawers to separate projects. How simple. We were told to keep a clean desk with only one project on it at a time. Yeah, right! "Not in my world," I thought.

I told my staff, "Never touch anything on my desk." I had a system. Everything important was on my desk... somewhere.

My constant searching through a pile of notes assured me that nothing would escape my attention. What a system. Now I wonder how much time I wasted looking for this or that.

I've not yet reached the "one project on the desk at a time" level of organization, but I have become much more organized. I spend less time looking for things. I forget fewer things.

Organization frees your mind so you can focus on what you are doing *now*. Computers store information that can be requested when needed. So can you.

**Organized people are more relaxed.
They have more time and less stress.
Make success easy; relax and enjoy the trip.**

Most people feel stress when they ask themselves, "Should I or shouldn't I?" Stress is fearing an answer you don't want to hear. You probably know what you should do. The right questions to ask are *how, when* or *where* you *can* do it.

Let's explore some other common success/failure programs. Remember: These programs are not suited for, or needed by, everyone.

 **You can be *whatever* you want to be.
Whatever you want to be is okay. "If the
shoe fits, wear it."**

With that thought in mind, here is a program that's high on the best seller list of "Goals and Excuses."

> **POSITIVE/SUCCESS PROGRAM:
> "How can I lose weight?"
> NEGATIVE/FAILURE PROGRAM:
> "I can't lose weight."**

The negative/failure program results in: "So why should I do without French fries, ice cream, candy or beer?" As long as you believe you can't lose weight, why suffer? Right? **Wrong!**

People spend a lot of money on weight loss programs, then tell themselves, "I *can't* lose weight."

The problem is with two words: *can't* and *lose*. *Anyone* can lose weight, and *everyone* knows it. Asking yourself, "How *can* I lose weight?" will result in predictable answers. The answers will **make success easy**.

 Losing weight is easy: *eat less* and *move more*.

"Lose" is a negative word. No one likes to lose anything, even unwanted weight. Better questions to ask yourself are:

"How much do I want to weigh?"
"How much do I weigh now?"
"How can I reach and maintain my desired weight?"

These are easy questions to answer. When you ask yourself the right questions, **success is easy.**

Facing an unpleasant reality encourages you to change it. Hiding from it allows you to accept it.

A friend used to say, "If everyone had to come to the dinner table naked, there would be very few overweight people."

To maintain a desired weight, identify it, imagine it, then track your progress towards it.

I devised a simple chart years ago that keeps me from gaining unwanted weight. I step on the scale every day, then visually graph the results. This requires only 15 seconds a day, but it works on my mind all day long. My subconscious "jumps in" and orders the salad before I can consciously say, "French fries."

I don't suffer, because my subconscious allows me to treat myself on those days that I have a downward trend on the chart. I've made a direct connection in my mind between what I eat today and the picture on the chart tomorrow. The chart is **"The Boss."** I face **"The Boss"** every day.

 Keep your goal in mind, and ask the right questions. The right answers will come.

When the answers come, take action. The action you think of might be awkward or unusual for you, but take it anyway.

Reinforce your new action with positive affirmations. Give more thought time to success. Eventually, success will become a dominant thought. That's when it becomes a reality.

A good weight-maintenance thought trigger is:

"Nothing tastes as good as being thin feels."

Make that statement to yourself the next time you encounter a different "thought trigger" while passing the ice cream counter. Another positive "thought trigger" is:

"I'll wear tomorrow what I eat today."

Throw this "handful of sand" into a bucket of "Wow, that pie looks good" water. The pie looks better than the denial feels, but only at the instant you consider it. At that moment, you will either eat the pie and lose, or walk away from it and win.

Imagine wearing a smaller belt. Take control – ask yourself, "What can I do, right now, this minute, to get closer to wearing a smaller belt?" You'll get an answer. When you do, take action. Walk away from the pie, and into the smaller belt. **It's easy.**

You are always moving towards success, or away from it.

"For whoever has,
*to him shall **more** be given,*
and he shall have an abundance;
but whoever does not have,
even what he has shall be taken away from him."
JESUS
MATTHEW 13:12

POSITIVE/SUCCESS PROGRAM:
"How can I master this job?"
NEGATIVE/FAILURE PROGRAM:
"I hate this job."

It's surprising how many people go through life working at a job they hate. They invest 40 or more hours a week of their God-given time doing something they do not want to do. As they do it, they tell themselves, "I hate this job." They get up in the morning and say, "Damn, I *have* to go to work!"

When you tell yourself that you *have* to go to work, you send two messages to your subconscious: "I *have* to do something I do not *want* to do, and it's work!"

You begin to dislike work. Work becomes a "four-letter word." You subconsciously avoid it. You move away from success.

I ask groups of people, "Is anyone here serving a prison sentence? Did a judge order you to work 40 hours a week for this company?" No one answers, "Yes."

You do not *have* to go to work.

Life is too short to spend time doing anything you don't *want* to do. People who hate their jobs should do one of two things: think differently about their job, or say two words: **"I quit."**

People who stay on a job they hate long enough eventually may hear: **"You're fired."**

"I quit," or "You're fired" can set off a barrage of new thoughts.

 Say, "I *get* to go to work."

Replace the word *"have"* with *"get"*, and you change the entire feeling. The message to your subconscious becomes powerful and positive. Work is a privilege.

Some people lose a job before realizing they really want it. When told "You're fired," some people beg for their jobs back. They promise to do their jobs better. They are willing to make a major attitude shift after it's too late.

Constantly telling yourself, "I *get* to go to work," reminds you that work is a privilege.

It makes success easy.

Many people stay on jobs or in relationships they hate because they fear change. If you can't change jobs, change how you do your job. Ask yourself, "What could I be *doing* right *now*, this minute, to *improve* my job?"

The biggest word in this question is "**I**." You are the only person who can make your job better.

 The best way to escape a job you don't like is to excel at it.

Companies look for excellence at every level, and when they discover it, they promote it. If you're doing a job you hate, maybe you're bored with it. Maybe you're bored because you know the job so well. Maybe you could do it half asleep. Maybe you do.

 Adding motivation to experience produces excellence.

Excellence leads to promotion. Continuous promotion eventually leads the brightest people into more challenging arenas. If you're bored, **get busy**.

POSITIVE/SUCCESS PROGRAM:
"How can I find more time to exercise?"
NEGATIVE/FAILURE PROGRAM:
"I don't have time to exercise."

The negative/failure program causes you to say, "... So I won't." No time – no exercise.

 One who wants to, finds a way;
one who doesn't, finds an excuse.

It's okay to not exercise, it's your choice. But, don't blame time when you don't. Time is not at fault. Time is limited to 24 hours a day, everyday. Time is constant. It never changes. It's the same for everyone.

Ask yourself, "How *can* I find more time to exercise?" You may not have time to exercise, but you do move. When you move, you exercise, even if it is just to get up from watching TV to walk to the refrigerator.

When you ask yourself, "How *can* I exercise more?" your subconscious accepts that you *do* exercise. To exercise more is easy. **Move more.**

If your exercise of choice is a formal activity such as running or aerobics, and considerable time is required, ask:

*"How can I find **more time** to ... ?"*

The amount of time you exercise is less important than the habit you are creating.

Exercising a minute or two every day is better than nothing. Devote one minute every day to a new exercise, and see what happens. The benefits will cause the minute to expand. Some less valuable activity will be displaced.

When you think about not having time to exercise, think about past presidents of the United States. Could you keep up with them?

Past presidents have jogged, swum and played touch football. They have enjoyed tennis and golf, and vacationed with their families while traveling the world, hosting banquets, attending dinners and meeting with world leaders and members of the Congress and Senate.

How do they find the time to jog? They do! They have 24 hours every day. So do you.

Ask yourself, "How can I find *more time* to exercise?" The answer will come. Reinforce your new intentions with affirmations. Tell yourself:

"Every minute I exercise makes me stronger."

In December of 1983 I stood at the finish line of the Honolulu Marathon and watched 10,000 people "finish." It was a moving experience.

The first finishers were world-class athletes. As they crossed the finish line, they calmly looked at their watches, strolled through the "finishers' showers", then relaxed and compared their "times."

The masses who crossed the finish line several hours later hobbled to the showers, lay on the grass, and walked very slowly. The last ones dragged themselves across the finish line and collapsed in the showers.

Everyone had one thing in common: they "finished." They had a common look on their faces. **Success.**

They had just run 26.2 miles. Some ran it in slightly more than two hours; others in 10 hours.

Some were 10 years old, some 20, some 80. They came in all sizes and shapes. They all got a T-shirt that said "Finisher." It didn't say how long it took them to finish. They were all *equal.*

They made it look **easy.**

I was jealous. I thought, "If they can do it, I can do it!" I had never run farther than three miles at one time in my life, but I believed that I was in better condition than many of the runners I watched crossing the finish line.

Did I have the time to train for a marathon? Did I have the desire? Was I willing to make the commitment I sensed it would take? I wanted to feel what those 10,000 people felt. I decided to go for it.

I had a year to prepare. I needed a plan. I needed a "vision." I photographed runners in the "finishers' showers." I put the pictures on the wall in my living room. I looked at the pictures and imagined myself taking a "finisher's shower" on December 9, 1984.

On January 1, 1984, I put my plan into effect. I lived along the marathon course, about a mile and a half from the finish line. My plan was to get up an hour earlier than usual each day, run to the finish line and back home, a three-mile workout. Every day I would go a little beyond the finish line to lengthen my run slightly. Every day I would look at the picture on the wall. Every day I would experience "finishing." Every day it would get **easier.**

I bought a journal and logged my progress. Everything in my plan was reasonable. All I had to do was start. I could **see success.**

My morning run gradually got longer. Every time I ran across the finish line I imagined myself in the "finishers' showers" on December 9. My morning ritual progressed steadily from three miles to five miles.

At this point, I entered a 10K race, six-and-two-tenths miles. I finished and got my first "finisher" T-shirt. I ran 25 or 30 more 10K races that year. These races became my Sunday workout. It was fun. **It was easy.**

Every time, I experienced crossing the finish line and receiving a "finisher" T-shirt. Every time, I imagined crossing the Marathon finish line on December 9.

My daily workout extended beyond five miles, to seven, then 10 miles. About half-way through the year, I entered a half-marathon, 13.1 miles. At the end of that race, I asked myself, "Could I turn around and run it again?" The answer was a resounding "**No!**"

I knew I wasn't ready yet. I ran four half-marathons that year, each one with a faster time. My confidence grew. **It was easy.**

As my morning workouts got longer, I woke up earlier and earlier. I found the time to run and loved the experience. In September I entered an 18-mile race. At the end of that race, I was ready to quit. **I didn't.**

In November I attempted a 20-mile training run. It went great. I imagined myself running another six-and-two-tenths miles. At last, I could see the light at the end of the tunnel.

A marathon is simply a 20-mile training run followed by a 10K race. I had now run a 20-mile training run, four half-marathons and 25 or more 10K races. I thought: "Piece of cake... **success will be easy.**"

My morning training run occupied one or two hours every day. The marathon became my dominant thought. I did my job, but I was "living to run."

My self-paradigm had shifted. I had become an athlete. I was no longer on the sidelines. I was a participant. I didn't need the long legs. I built the big muscles. I was ready.

It was easy.

It rained all night before the marathon. Imagine 12,000 runners with trash bags over their heads waiting to start a 26-mile foot race.

We had 40 m.p.h. headwinds for the first 18 miles of the race. At the 22-mile mark, I felt like a million dollars. At the 24-mile mark, I wanted to quit. That's where the image of the "finishers' showers" entered my mind and motivated me to complete the remaining 2.2 miles.

I finished in 4 hours 36 minutes. I missed my goal by 6 minutes, but I "finished." Success is sweet; I got my T-shirt.

The "finishers'" shower felt so good I didn't want to leave. A minute or two later, I sat down in a lawn chair. Five minutes later I couldn't get up. It was several days before I could walk normally. I realized that my leg muscles were shot long before I reached the finish line. Mind over matter carried me the last few miles.

It was easy.

POSITIVE/SUCCESS PROGRAM:
"How can I stop smoking?"
NEGATIVE/FAILURE PROGRAM:
"I can't stop smoking."

I grew up detesting cigarette smoke. Both of my parents and all of my relatives smoked. When I became a teenager, I argued with my parents about their smoking. My dad said, "I can't quit. Someday you'll understand."

I entered the Air Force as an 18-year-old confirmed non-smoker; I came out smoking Camels. I'd heard stories about the military encouraging smoking, but I did not think they would get me.

It started in basic training. After a long march, the drill sergeant would call out: "Smoke 'em if you got 'em." Those who smoked would "fall out" and relax.

The rest of us had to wait until the smokers were finished. The smokers joked and smoked. They were "cool." One by one, the non-smokers became smokers.

I started smoking. I told myself that I would quit soon and show my father how easy quitting is.

What I thought would be easy was one of the hardest things I've ever done. In the process of quitting, I gained great respect for the power of this habit. But, it *can* be conquered. **It's easy.**

The hardest thing I've ever done was the easiest.

To quit smoking I didn't have to *do* anything. I just had to *not do* one thing.

I started asking myself, "How can I stop smoking?" The answer came back: "DON'T PUT ANY CIGA-RETTES IN YOUR MOUTH, NOT ONE MORE!" **Easy!**

I read articles on how to quit smoking and I tried to stop many times. In the final analysis, it all came down to me. Did I want to be a smoker? No! Then don't light up, period! **It's easy.**

Smokers see themselves as smokers – it's their self-image. If you want to quit smoking, then change your habit. Change your perception. Support your desire to stop smoking with positive affirmations. Say:

> *"I like being a non-smoker."*

Start *non-smoking* rather than stop smoking. **It's easy.**

As the new self-image of a *non-smoker* emerges, support it. Say:

> *"I breathe deeply, I smell the flowers,*
> *and taste my food."*

POSITIVE/SUCCESS PROGRAM:
"How can I make today a great day?"
NEGATIVE/FAILURE PROGRAM:
"It's going to be one of those days."

What are *"those days"* anyway? You know! It's easy to hang a label on a day. A few disappointments early in the day can cause you to see the entire day as a disaster. Your mental data bank knows what you mean by *"one of those days."* When you tell yourself it's going to be *"one of those days,"* your subconscious thinks you want one. It delivers it.

 Words and thoughts are powerful.

Ask yourself questions that demand answers you want. Ask:

"How can I make this a great day?"

The answer will come. Say:

"This is another great day... success awaits me."

 You bring about what you think about. To have great days, expect great days. It's easy.

POSITIVE/SUCCESS PROGRAM:
"How can I save more money?"
NEGATIVE/FAILURE PROGRAM:
"I can't save any money."

Telling yourself that you *can't* save any money gives you permission to spend it all. You *can't* save any, so, why not splurge? Right? **Wrong!**

Remember this:

> *"It's easier to get by on what's left after saving,*
> *than to save what's left after getting by."*

Small amounts of money saved meticulously won't be missed. Small deposits into a savings account become large amounts over the years. You *can* save money.

Like everything else, saving starts in the mind. *How much* you save is unimportant. It is important that you save *some*, routinely. Ask yourself, "How *can* I save more money?" The answers will come. When they do, act, affirm, believe and save.

It's easy.

POSITIVE/SUCCESS PROGRAM:
"What can I do?"
NEGATIVE/FAILURE PROGRAM:
"I don't know what to do."

If you tell yourself that you don't know what to do, you won't do anything. Instead, ask yourself:

"What can I do?"

You *can* overcome any obstacle you encounter in life. Any pain *can* be healed. Any problem *can* be solved.
It's easy.

There are *problem-solvers* and *problem-makers*. *Problem-solvers* make more money, have less stress and are more successful. Be a *problem-solver*.
It's easy.

One who looks for problems finds them...
One who looks for solutions finds them.
PROBLEMS ARE OPPORTUNITIES IN
DISGUISE.

Get excited when someone says, "I've got a problem." Many wonderful opportunities are revealed by solving a problem.

Say:

"Every problem has a solution. I am a problem-solver,
so problems are good."

Replace *can't* with *can,* *won't* with *will* and *if* with *when.*

Convince yourself that you *can* have what you *want,* then ask yourself, *"How?"* As the course of action is revealed to you, *act!* Action displaces inaction.

It's tempting to wait until you *feel* like taking action.

 Feelings follow action – action does not follow feelings.

If you wait until you *feel* like doing something, you may never do it. A good example is getting out of bed in the morning. What if you lay there until you *felt* like getting up?

I have found that regardless of how badly I want to stay in bed, I am only a few steps away from a different feeling. Once I make it to the shower, I know I will make it through the day. Confucius said,

"A journey of 1,000 miles begins with a single step."

 The time spent deciding to do something is better spent doing it.

Nike has a great affirmation: "JUST DO IT." W. Clement Stone says, "DO IT NOW." These are good statements to make when you catch yourself putting off doing something.

The "snooze button" is a popular feature on many alarm clocks. It allows you to go back to sleep when you should get up.

I've tried the "snooze button," but I noticed a poorer quality of sleep after being awakened. I know people who set their alarm to go off 30 minutes before they have to get up just so they can hit the "snooze button" three or four more times.

Get rid of the "snooze buttons" in your life.

 Just do it.
Do it now!
Make success easy.

Chapter 5

Stuff Happens–
Success Follows

"Life is just God watching television."
DEAN POGNI – 7 YEARS OLD

Attitude affects behavior. Behavior determines results. To make success easy, control your attitude and success will follow. Life is full of "emotional torpedoes." I call them *life's little situations.*

All too often, people let their emotions dictate their life, which resembles a roller coaster ride of soaring highs and sinking lows.

Imagine that you have two big faucets somewhere in your stomach. Each faucet controls the flow of stomach juices that inspire or paralyze you at emotional times.

When the positive faucet is open, you feel supercharged, tingling with confidence and excitement. Conversely, when something negative happens, the other faucet opens up. It releases negative, paralyzing juices into your stomach.

These juices influence your behavior. You feel motivated and invincible or helpless and doomed, depending on which faucet is open. Your subconscious responds to your emotions.

Many times it seems as though you have no control over these faucets. Something happens to you, and one of the faucets opens automatically.

Imagine going to your mailbox and finding a letter from your insurance company. The letter explains that there was a computer error and says, "Please find our check for $10,000."

As you imagine finding this check in your mailbox, which stomach faucet opens up? You look at the check and see yourself spending the money. You feel great. It's going to be a great day.

Now imagine a different envelope in your mailbox. This one is from the I.R.S. It says, "You owe $10,000. Please remit your check immediately."

Now which faucet opens up? It's a challenge to be positive and excited when you don't like what's happening to you. Take control of these two faucets in your stomach. **Make success easy.**

You have no control over your "mailbox of life." Stuff happens. You *can* control how you react. When something frightens you, and the negative juices begin to paralyze you, take control. Shut that faucet off, and open the other one. **You can do it! It's easy!**

Successful people work with what they have and get what they want.

The positive/successful person might wisely invest the $10,000 windfall and turn it into $100,000. That same person may use the $10,000 IRS demand as motivation to increase his or her income, and maybe turn it into $100,000 in the process.

Negative/failures might accept the $10,000 check and then "blow it." The $10,000 debt might cause them to "blow their brains out." One person's good news is another person's bad news.

Let's explore some of *life's little situations.*

Change is Good

Change deserves its place at the head of this list. Most people fear and resist change, even when it is good.

 Make change your friend.

You can't avoid change. It is the only true constant in life. Change will come, and in a variety of forms.

Change is as sure as the rising sun. It can be as beautiful as a rainbow or as ravaging as a hurricane. You cannot predict its form, only its presence.

Change is ominous. Make change your friend.

Let's say the boss walks into a room full of employees and announces: "Things are going to change around here." Everyone's stomach faucets open up. One group *cheers*: "Great, what are we going to do?" The other group *fears*: "Oh no, what are we going to do?" One group is excited about the upcoming change... the other is fearful of it. Yet no one has heard the change.

Changes are self-imposed and externally-imposed. Some changes you control; others control you. You can control your emotions regardless.

Self-imposed changes require bold thinking, planning, courage and time. Externally-imposed changes can hit you in an instant. You may not have time to plan or think. Sometimes you have no choice at all. Sometimes the change looks bad.

People say, "Everything happens for the best." That sounds good, but at the moment of change, you might fear the unknown. You don't know what's going to happen next, and that's scary.

 You don't have to know what's going to happen next, only that it will be good.

To calm yourself down, say:

"This too is good, and soon I'll know why."

Three externally-imposed changes molded my life. Given my choices, I would not have made any of these three changes. Each change forced me to grow and succeed. Each change caused me pain and stress. The second one changed me the most. It also hurt me the most.

Major Life Change #1

It was November 1980. I was a co-owner of a million-dollar-a-month company. I was married to Terri. We lived on a seven-acre mountaintop estate overlooking Southern California. I drove Cadillacs, she drove Porsches.

Terri loved animals. At last count we had 13 cats and seven dogs, including two Great Danes. We also had 15 birds, exotic and common. Everything was perfect. Life was good. I would have "freeze-framed" my life right there. It couldn't be better.

One evening Terri said, "We need to talk." I'll never forget her next words: "I don't want to be married anymore."

I felt as though I had been hit by a train that I didn't see coming. I thought everything was wonderful. We never argued throughout our eight-year marriage.

I was always preaching positive thinking and self-control to my employees. My office walls were covered with positive "thought triggers" to defend me against anything negative. I had overcome huge obstacles to succeed. Now, I felt helpless. My positive affirmations abandoned me. My mind filled with fear and self-pity. I begged to know why. When she told me, I begged for forgiveness. When she refused, I cried.

I sold my business to my partner the next day, and cried for the next five months. I was pitiful. Paralyzing juices poured through my stomach day and night. I pictured a life of misery and loneliness.

I told myself I would never be able to replace Terri. I felt betrayed and abandoned, angry and victimized. But I took no responsibilities.

Eventually I realized that I had brought this miserable change upon myself. I was so obsessed with my business that I had neglected my wife. I no longer did the "little things." I was too busy to tell her how pretty she was, too busy to bring home flowers, or too busy to take vacations.

I was too busy for my own success.

 Once I accepted responsibility, change became good.

I started thinking about the future. Now I was free to do anything I wanted to do. I would not have sold my business, but I did. I would never have left my wife and home, but they were gone.

I always enjoyed visiting Hawaii. I had often talked with Terri about living in Hawaii. Our conversation always ended with the thought of moving our "zoo" to Hawaii.

I no longer lived in the "zoo." I *could* move to Hawaii. I took action. I bought a one-way ticket. I "flew the coop."

My feelings changed. Life began to flow in my veins. I selected May lst to move to Hawaii. May Day is Lei Day in Hawaii – everyone wears flowers. It was a special day for me. It still is.

I rented a penthouse condominium in Waikiki, bought a surfboard and took surfing lessons. Within a matter of days, I was lying on my surfboard, looking at breathtaking sunsets and rainbows. I began to feel really good. **Feelings follow action.**

The next eight years were "pure paradise." I owe it to Terri for having the courage to make the change. Someday I'll repay her.

Now I was living in a beach house on the North Shore of Oahu. I owned another new Cadillac, and I rediscovered success. I was the senior vice president of a major Hawaii retailer and, best of all, I was married to Sarah.

Sarah was the kindest, most beautiful woman alive. An angel on earth. Everyone loved her, especially me. Once again I would have opted for a life "freeze-frame." It couldn't get any better than this.

Major life change #2

Sarah was young, strong and beautiful. I knew she had Lupus, but I didn't know it was a deadly disease. I never dreamed it would kill her. How could I deal with this?

My dad used to say, "The good die young." Those words filled my mind. I asked myself over and over, "Why... Why... Why?" I still haven't received the right answer.

Sarah was barely 30 years old. She was healthy and fit. She competed in triathlons. How could she die?

When Sarah was stricken, all of my priorities shifted instantly. She spent four months in and out of Intensive Care. So did I.

I met some real heroes and heroines in the Intensive Care Unit. I noticed major differences between them and their colleagues on other floors of the hospital. The dominant thought in Intensive Care is to preserve life. Nothing is overlooked.

On the other floors, the medical staff focus more on the technical job they are doing than on the patients they are doing it for. Patients are merely part of the process. In Intensive Care, patients are the purpose.

Intensive Care has rules. No one can stay for more than 10 minutes. I wouldn't hear of it. I barged in, armed with pizza and chocolates. I had my way with the staff. I started thinking like the doctors. I found myself wishing I were a doctor so I could take over and save Sarah.

Soon, all that kept her alive was her strong heart. It wouldn't quit – Sarah didn't die easily. Her condition consumed all of my thinking until the very end.

We held the funeral at our home on the beach. Intensive Care nurses attended. They see a lot of death, but rarely attend funerals.

I arranged to have a helicopter land on the lawn by the beach. It was the same helicopter we used for our wedding and honeymoon.

Her father, brothers and I flew her ashes to the cliffs of Moloka'i where Sarah and I declared our wedding vows two years earlier. I released her ashes and a helicopter full of flowers. As they drifted towards the ocean, I thought, "She is gone. I am left. What will I do now?"

Once again, my positive thinking abandoned me. I found myself walking the beach, crying out loud, and asking "Why... Why... Why?"

For the first time in 15 years, I didn't want to go to work; I didn't. Day after day, I walked the beach Sarah and I had walked together so many times. I wandered around our big empty house, looking at photographs.

The only person I welcomed was Sarah's mother, my sweet Schatzie. We held each other and cried. Schatzie was a daily visitor, my only visitor.

I became reclusive. I didn't want anyone to interrupt my constant asking of "Why?" I kept asking myself a question I couldn't answer. I still can't answer it. I still ask it.

I saw myself as a lonely beach bum. I hadn't shaved since the day Sarah died, so I looked the part. All I did was walk the beach. I knew I would never be the same.

In time I began to feel an obligation to return to work. I began to think: "*I have* to go to work."

Change #3

I returned to work against my will and hid behind my beard. I have heard that people with beards are hiding something. I don't believe that, but *I was.*

I thought if I put my body into the job, the old attitude would soon return. **Feelings follow action.**

"The Year Of The Beard" was a year of change. I came out of my "beach bum hibernation" with different priorities. I stepped into the same job I had stepped out of a few short months ago, but everything was different. It wasn't fun anymore. I wasn't fun anymore.

The company had recently been sold. The original owner had an entrepreneurial style. He and I worked together like partners.

The new owners emphasized M & M's: meetings and memos.

While married to Sarah, I was oblivious to the subtle changes being imposed upon me at work. I knew I was being underutilized, but I tolerated it. I sat in long meetings watching people make "big deals" out of "small things" they really didn't care about.

Nothing had changed, except me. I had changed dramatically. My priorities were different. Time was precious. I couldn't tolerate low-level discussions, even at the highest level in the company. Life was too precious to waste doing anything meaningless.

I refused to waste precious moments on office politics. I stopped picking and choosing my words. I skipped meetings that I knew were going to waste my time. I began looking at my job as something I *had* to do rather than something I *got* to do.

The new owners held me in what they laughingly called their "Golden Handcuffs," my generous compensation package. I was being paid too much to quit. I would have to walk away from a million-dollar annuity agreement.

I've since learned that "All that glitters is not gold."

 No amount of money is sufficient to waste your precious time on earth.

Most people would not "sit in jail" for any amount of money. People in jail would spend big money to get out.

Some people "sit in jail" at work. I "broke out" of jail once when I quit my job 25 years ago, and here I was right back in it.

I had accepted my "Golden Handcuffs" even though they were tarnishing. I was going through the motions and taking the money, just like everyone else.

 When change is imperative for your own good, and you don't make it consciously, then your subconscious takes over and makes the change for you.

The company president was a good friend. He took me to lunch and announced, "Things are going to change in the company. I don't think you'll like the new direction, and you might want to consider a change for yourself." He opened the "jail door" for me to walk out. He also opened up the negative faucet in my stomach.

I asked, "What's going to change?" He said that the owners want to concentrate more on profits than sales. He suspected they would change the commissions I was paying to my salespeople, and eliminate many of the prize and bonus programs I had created over the past 10 years.

My negative reaction became defensive. I pointed out that the "pennies" I spent produced millions of dollars for the company. He said he understood, and even agreed, but these changes were beyond his control. It was either play the new game, or move on.

I shaved my face and moved on.

It was easy–It was good.

In a few short years I was paying myself many times what any one company could pay me, and no M & M's. I didn't need the annuity policy; I *earned* the million dollars. **It was easy.**

Criticism Is Positive

Most people are too easy on themselves. They get upset when someone points out their faults. The negative/failure reaction to criticism is to "defend and attack." People exclaim: "I didn't do that. Who said I did?"

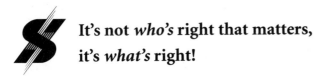 **It's not *who's* right that matters, it's *what's* right!**

Put your ego in your back pocket and search for your faults. Go on a **K.G.B.** mission – **Keep Getting Better.**

The better you get, the bigger the challenge is to *keep getting better.* As you become more successful, you may lose some of your motivation. You are not as hungry and you have corrected many of your faults. Your remaining faults might not be obvious to you.

You may need help. When someone points to a fault of yours, which faucet in your stomach opens up? If your initial response is defensive or argumentative, you might miss the value of the criticism.

When you get mad, or defensive, you block out objectivity.

Early in my business, I had a client who asked his employees to rate my presentation. He told them to be very honest, and that "Ron will never see this stuff."

He invited me to lunch and said, "Ron, you have to see this stuff." He told me, "This feedback is so valuable, you couldn't buy it." I said, "Okay, let's see it."

I read a flattering comment, smiled and nodded in agreement. Then I came across a critique that said, "I don't think he's very professional – he kept putting his hands in his pockets."

I stopped reading and exclaimed; "Wait a minute. I don't put my hands in my pockets. I know better." I got mad. I got defensive. I was being accused of doing something I knew I hadn't done. I said, "Who wrote this? Who is Laura?"

He sensed I was overreacting and tried to calm me down by saying, "She probably made a mistake." It ruined my lunch. I drove home thinking, "Wait till I see Laura, I'll tell her." The criticism stayed on my mind into the evening, "How dare she say such a thing!"

Eventually, a little voice told me: "You must have had your hands in your pockets." I began to realize that Laura had no reason to make this up. I must have picked up a bad habit somewhere along the way.

Criticism always helps, even if it is not valid. I still don't know if I had my hands in my pockets that day or not. I do know they haven't been in my pockets since.

It's not who's right that's important, but **what's** *right.*

 Dismiss your anger and diminish your ego when accepting criticism. Just say, "Thank you."

You don't have to agree with the criticism. Say "Thank you for mentioning it. I'll consider it." Or say, "Thank you for pointing that out to me. I'll work on it." Or just say, "Thank you."

It's easy.

Courtroom lawyers must stay civil while facing repeated criticism. When one lawyer declares, "Objection," everyone has to stop and wait for one of two words from the judge – "Overruled," or "Sustained." When the judge announces, "Objection overruled," the objecting attorney sits down, and the other attorney moves on.

When objections are sustained, the questioning attorneys must put their ego aside, change their course of questioning and move on. When lawyers let their egos get in the way, they are held in contempt.

People sometimes put themselves in contempt when they are criticized. They say, "No, not me."

When someone is willing to run the risk of offending you with criticism, be thankful. They say, "Only your best friends will tell you." When they do, say, "Thank you." **It's easy.**

 You will be exposed to changes and criticism–stuff happens. Both will make you more successful.

Praise is Rewarding

Praise feels good. The boss says, "You're doing a great job. You've got a bright future here." The positive/successful person will think: "Wow, you haven't seen anything yet. I know I'm not perfect, and if you're happy with me now, you're going to love me tomorrow because I'm going to *keep getting better.*"

Negative/failures hear praise, and let up. They catch T.I.A.D. (Thumb In Armpit Disease). Do you get the picture? They think: "I've got it made."

 Celebrate yesterday's success, but never at the expense of today's opportunity.

Take mental snapshots of your emotional reaction to praise and criticism. They both keep you on the track to **success.**

When your mental snapshot shows defense or anger, refocus and reshoot. When this becomes a habit you will crave criticism and savor praise. Make praise and criticism your friends.

They make success easy.

Welcoming Interruptions

While I was meeting with a successful retailer, his phone rang: He said, "Excuse me," and asked his secretary, "Does it involve a sale?" When she replied "Yes," he took the call and made the sale.

Then he returned his attention to me saying, "I make money with everything I do. That call made me money, and you make me money. Now, where were we?"

I was impressed. I didn't mind waiting for him to finish that important call. I felt his full attention when he resumed talking to me.

A co-worker might barge into your space and ask a question, or try to make small talk. It's easy to bark, "Can't you see I'm busy?," or offer a sigh and "eye roll" that says: "Whatever you want is not as important as what I was doing when you interrupted me."

Some of the most productive executives have an "open door policy." Most employees respect busy people and won't take advantage of them.

Executives with open doors willingly run the risk of interruptions in order to avoid the risk of not being asked a key question at a crucial moment.

Interruptions will happen regardless of whether you invite them or not. When they do, it is important to react positively. When someone says, "Excuse me," and you react: "What now?", you could damage your relationship with that person and not know the purpose of the interruption.

 Successful people change their focus without negative emotion or loss of intensity.

My father used to say, "When you feel torn in many directions, imagine a Big Ben clock in the middle of a hurricane. The windows are blowing in, the roof is coming loose, but old Big Ben keeps going tick... tick... tick."

When you feel stressed, say "tick.. tick... tick." When people are pulling at you from different directions, say "tick... tick... tick."

There was a dramatic point in the O.J. Simpson trial during a side-bar conference. Prosecutor Christopher Darden was *interrupted* by defense lawyer Johnnie

Cochran, who made a demeaning comment about the prosecutor's lack of experience in "cases such as this."

Darden exploded and the judge held him in contempt. With emotions raging, Darden denied his contempt and demanded counsel.

An *interruption* followed by an explosive emotional *response* caused the entire focus of the court to be changed from double murder to "lawyer ego."

Judge Lance Ito said, "Mr. Darden, I suggest you take a deep breath, as I am going to do, and contemplate your next remark." Darden's next remark was: "I don't have to think about it – I want counsel."

The judge wisely ordered a recess and invited Darden to read the transcript. Judge Ito said, "All you have to do, Mr. Darden, is apologize to the court, and we can continue."

During the recess, Chris Darden read the transcript and readily apologized to the court. It was over. The transcript contained his own words. He *was* in contempt.

People put themselves into "contempt" with their family and colleagues without realizing it. When someone interrupts you, and you feel your emotions boiling, follow Judge Lance Ito's sage advise: Take a deep breath, and contemplate your response.

It will **make success easy**.

Pressure Creates Growth

In sports they say: "He's a pressure player." In life we hear: "She works well under pressure." These are good reputations to have. Pressure can make or break you. Some people say, "I can't work under pressure."

Make pressure your friend.

When you feel pressure, remember that diamonds are made from relatively worthless chunks of carbon. When subjected to the earth's intense pressure, a chunk of carbon becomes a gem of great value.

 Pressure makes you do things you might not otherwise do. Pressure makes you try harder, think smarter and achieve more.

The boss says, "Pick up the pace." You have an unexpected expense. You are nearing your deadline on a project. You feel pressure.

Most of "life's little situations" create pressure. Positive/successful people benefit from externally imposed pressures. They also put pressure on themselves. Negative pressure is expressed in worry or fear. It can paralyze you. Positive pressure stimulates action.

It makes success easy.

 Do what you fear, and your fear will vanish. Action dissolves paralysis.

You may feel pressure because you don't know how to solve a problem. Maybe you can't visualize the complete path to success.

You don't have to know every step to take. Begin by taking the first step, then the next, and the next. You will find the path as long as you keep moving forward with a positive attitude.

You don't need to know *how* you will solve the problem, just that you *will*.

Remember, *feelings follow action*. When you *feel* pressure, take *action*. You'll *feel* motivated.

 Failure Leads To Success

"Failure lies in waiting for someone to embrace it."

Thomas Edison failed 10,000 times in his quest to invent the electric light bulb. He didn't give up. He said, "I am 10,000 experiments closer to success." The world has benefitted greatly from one man's refusal to accept failure.

Think and Grow Rich author Napoleon Hill wrote, "Within every adversity lies the seed of an equal, or greater benefit." W. Clement Stone added, "for those with a positive mental attitude."

When you see failure as a step towards success, you will keep moving. To fail is to quit or give up. When thoughts of failure find their way into your mind, displace them immediately.

**Failure is only success in disguise.
Ask yourself,"What can I do right now,
this minute, to change this situation?"
Ask "What is good about this situation?"
or "How can I make this failure a success?"**

A young inventor at the Minnesota Mining Company was trying to create a stronger adhesive. He failed. His final product barely stuck paper together. Without trying he invented the adhesive material for Post-It note cards.

The world now uses these colorful little stickers instead of stapling or clipping notes. And it's all because of one man's failure. This is success made of "failure."

**Making decisions right is more important
than making right decisions. Be persistent!**

Successful people can recount past failures. Some will brag that their failures earned them millions of dollars. Others will say that failures taught them the most valuable lessons in their life. Some say:

"If not for failure, I surely would have failed."

You accept failure when you quit. When you quit, you are finished.

Winners never quit; quitters never win!

Quitters say, "I tried." They tell you; "It didn't work."

Say: "If at first I don't succeed, I'll try, try again." There is wisdom in quotes and tales that pass the test of time.

Practice W. Clement Stone's R^2A^2 principle. When confronted with failure, ask yourself, "What should I be learning?" Ask: "How can I use this situation to my advantage?"

Think about the "The Little Train That Could." It said, "I think I can, I think I can." Eventually those words became "I know I can, I know I can." That story has passed the test of time.

The negative/failure says: "If the engine on my choo-choo dies, and it won't restart, it's not my fault."

Positive/successful people ask: "What *can* I do to get to the top of that hill?" They get a different answer. They take a different action. Their feelings change. They *run* to the top of the hill, or attract a *new* choo-choo, or maybe they catch a *jet.*

One who wants to, finds a way;
one who doesn't, finds an excuse.

Imagine that you are in the "stream of life." You are trying to swim upstream to a nicer place. Upstream there are tall trees and crystal clear pools. It's plush and serene.

Downstream it's polluted and congested. The pools are murky and smelly. Get the point? That's why you are swimming.

You get tired and rest in one of the pools. Soon you must swim again. You feel the temptation to just tread water for a while.

You forget that the next pool upstream will be worth the swim. You cannot tread water forever. You cannot freeze-frame life. You have to keep swimming. If you stop too long, the current will wash you back.

My dad told me: "Just point your nose to the sun and take the next step."

Success Leads To Success

Success can be rewarding or devastating. How you see success determines your potential for more.

Everyone enjoys some success. Even a blind hog gets an acorn now and then.

 Respect success. It will multiply.

See every success as the tip of the iceberg. Discover the rest.

It's easy.

Never say: "I got lucky." If it's okay to *credit* good luck for your successes, then it's also okay to *blame* bad luck for your failures.

When you catch yourself saying, "I got lucky," you should immediately add:

> *"The harder I work, the luckier I get," or*
> *"The best way to find luck is to look for it."*

How about:

> *"Success is only luck... ask any failure."*

Accept full responsibility for your successes as well as for your failures.

Say, **"I did it once, I can do it again."** It's hard to argue with that.

 Tell yourself, "If one blade of grass grows here, I can have a lawn."

Spreading Good News

I once heard someone say: "I don't know whether to read the newspaper in the morning and ruin my day, or watch the news at night and ruin my sleep."

We live in a negative society. Bad news sells! It sells newspaper space. It sells television and radio time. It sells you "thought time."

Let's say you're driving to work. You notice a beautiful sunrise or rainbow on one side, and a wreck on the other side. Which one will you look at? Which one will you talk about when you get to work?

People are more likely to talk about the wrecks they witness than their sunrises, sunsets and rainbows. If you search the newspaper, you will find some positive stories, but the negative ones get more attention, and are more likely to become "water cooler talk."

Notice how perky some sick people become when you ask them how they feel. You hear gross details that make you wish you hadn't asked. When those same people feel great they say: "I'm okay," or, "Not too bad."

People say, "Not too bad" when they mean good, or even great. Saying, "Not too bad" on the great days tells your subconscious that all days are "bad," some are "not *too* bad." Your words **make success easy**.

Tell everyone you are "great." Tell yourself you are "great" every chance you get.

Look for good news, then spread it around.

Become selective about which topics you will discuss.

If a friend visited your home and started tossing garbage around your living room, would you tolerate it? No! So, don't let anyone throw garbage in your mind.

Keep the garbage out. **Make success easy.**

Chapter 6

Road Maps
To Success

"Goals are to success what road maps are to driving."

Can you imagine jumping into your car and driving off without a destination? Many people approach life this way – spending more time planning their vacations than planning their lives.

When the subject of goals comes up, some people roll their eyes and think, "Oh no, not goal-setting again." When I speak about goal-setting, I camouflage the title of the program. I call it "Reaching For The Stars."

My dad used to say,

*"If you reach for the stars, you won't get
any mud in your hands."*

Reasonable and *attainable* goals will motivate you to higher achievement. *Reasonable* and *attainable* goals will guide you to **success**.

A person without a goal is like a ship without a rudder.

Without a steering mechanism, a boat might travel in circles or run aground. Has that ever happened to you? Have you ever asked yourself, "How did I get here?"

You can approach an airline counter, buy a ticket, and fly anywhere in the world. There's one catch. You have to know where you want to go. The counter attendant will ask, "What's your destination?" If you don't know, you must step out of line and let others move ahead. And you must stay out of line until you decide where you want to go.

It's that way in life, too. You stay where you are until you decide where you want to go.

 People who know where they are going get there.

Many people resist goal-setting. Companies therefore set goals for people. At times *imposed* goals may seem unfair, unrealistic or unattainable. A goal deemed unreachable is non-existent.

Self-imposed goals can be as easy as you choose them to be.

You can set yourself up to be a winner. Here's how: Give yourself an easy goal that insures success. You may need a "taste of success."

 You can start with an easy goal, experience success, then raise your goal a little higher.

Your subconscious records every goal-reaching experience. Your goals become targets you *expect* to hit. You *can* have anything you *want;* just target it.

It's easy.

Have you ever wondered how trainers teach whales to jump over a black bar held high out of the water? They start by placing the black bar on the bottom of the tank. Get the idea? Even the dumbest and laziest whales eventually swim over the black bar. When they do, the trainers celebrate. They blow whistles and throw fish.

At first the whales have no idea what triggered this excitement and reward. In time, it happens again, then again. Every time the whales cross the bar, the whistles are blown and the fish are thrown.

Some whales catch on quicker than others, but eventually they all make the connection. Cross the bar, get the whistles and fish. Once this is learned, the whales swim back and forth over the bar repeatedly.

Now the trainers begin raising the bar, slowly and systematically. One day the bar is high enough so the whales can swim over or under it. The whales learn that only by swimming over the bar do they get the whistles and fish.

When the bar is finally raised above the water level, the whales jump over it. The bar eventually is raised higher out of the water than the whales would ever jump in their entire life. They make the jump. Get the idea? So can you.

Success is easy.

My father told me a story about a farmer who picked up a newborn calf and placed it over his shoulders. He picked it up the next day and every day until the calf grew into a full-grown steer.

As the calf gained weight, the farmer gained strength. The farmer never doubted his ability. He always knew he could pick up the calf. "I picked him up yesterday... I can pick him up today." The weight was a non-issue. **It was easy.**

Reward yourself when you achieve your goal. Give yourself the "whistles and fish."

Predetermine specific rewards like: new clothes for lost weight, vacations for added income, or dinner at a restaurant for finishing a project.

Keep the rewards coming, and keep raising the goal. You will **Keep Getting Better, K. G. B.**

Goals communicate with your subconscious.

Goals turn dreams into reality. When you find your-self dreaming about having something, going some-where, or doing something, it can be a reality or just a dream. Time passes by either way.

Goals give you *motivation* and *focus*.

Motivation

I learned the meaning of motivation in a dramatic fashion. It was in my junior high school gym class. I have forgotten the teacher's name but recall the message clearly.

The year was 1954. Juvenile controls were consider-ably harsher then. Today, they would be considered child abuse.

Most teachers at my school kept paddles in their desks. Various classroom disruptions would merit a cer-tain number of "swats."

The offender walked solemnly to the head of the class and bent over while the teacher applied the pun-ishment. The "swats" were painful and humiliating.

Some teachers enjoyed swatting us, while others dreaded it. Shop teachers were the most feared of all. They used custom paddles made of hard wood or plas-tic. Their paddles had strategically drilled holes in them to enhance air speed, velocity and impact.

One shop teacher's wall displayed 50 paddles. Each paddle had a name and number. The number referred to how many "swats" you would get. The name was something you would remember. You could pick your own paddle.

"Big Bertha" was a two-handed model about two-and-a-half feet long. She carried only one swat. To my knowledge, no one ever picked "Big Bertha."

In contrast, the librarian used a small ping pong paddle and swung it with very little conviction. The tough boys would "act up" in the library, hoping to provoke a paddling.

Some boys put magazines in their pants for extra padding. They howled in mock pain, while the class roared in laughter. Everyone enjoyed it except the poor librarian. She knew this was negative motivation.

On our first day of Physical Education, the gym teacher told us to strip naked and stand shoulder-to-shoulder. He unveiled his paddle: "Mr. Motivation." I'm sure he put in some late-night hours with the shop teacher engineering this fearsome weapon.

The gym teacher asked us if we understood what the word motivation meant. Few did. He explained: "When I tell you to do something, and you do it half-heartedly, you need motivation. "Mr. Motivation" will get you to do what I ask you to do when you don't want to."

He spoke about "Mr. Motivation" and the philosophy of motivation for several minutes. It seemed like several days.

He kept waving "Mr. Motivation" in front of us. He told us that anytime we needed some extra motivation, "Mr. Motivation" was there to help. He told us to remember this when we are out on the field. He said that any "swats" we earned on the field would be applied in the locker room, naked! So much for a magazine in the pants.

I felt motivated already. The gym teacher asked us to extend our arms, touching fingertips to fingertips. Then he barked, "Turn around and grab your ankles." He said: "I want you to remember the sting of "Mr. Motivation."

That was over 40 years ago, and I still remember the sting of "Mr. Motivation." I was not a star athlete in junior high school, but whatever I lacked in physical skill, I made up for in *motivation*.

I never felt the sting of "Mr. Motivation" again. Some of the most physically talented students had regular sessions with "Mr. Motivation." I thought they were tough. I later realized they were lazy. All they lacked was motivation.

Any teacher that used "Mr. Motivation" or "Big Bertha" on our kids today, would go to jail and rightly so. It *would* be child abuse.

Negative motivation can work. It worked on me, but it's not good motivation. It hurts, and it doesn't work on everyone.

Trainers never have to beat the whale. The whale swims over the bar for rewards. Affection training has replaced the whip and chair in training wild animals.

The art of motivation has evolved. Today, *goals* provide positive motivation that feels good, and lasts longer.

Focus

You can start a fire on a sunny day with dry paper and a magnifying glass. You must hold the magnifying glass very still, focusing the sun's energy onto the paper. The finer the focus, the faster the fire.

You can use a *very* big magnifying glass on a *very* hot day, with *very* dry paper, and be unable to start a fire unless you hold the magnifying glass *very* still.

Like the magnifying glass, your mind must be *focused* in order to build the "fire of desire" inside yourself.

 Focus on your goal until it burns a path into your subconscious.

Distinguish between goals that work *for you* and goals that work *on you*. Goals that work *on you* are usually externally-imposed. Sometimes these goals seem unrealistic or unreachable. They can create stress and might cause you to abandon your goal.

Goals that work *for you* drive you stress-free over or around any obstacles. You become internally driven towards success.

The difference between these two types of goals is acceptance by your subconscious. If you feel stress or fear, remind yourself that you are better than you think you are.

 When your subconscious focuses on your goal, magic happens.

For your goal to be accepted by your subconscious, it must be **SPECIFIC**. Avoid these words when goal setting:

"About"

"If"

"Try"

For example, the word "about" can be significant. Consciously, you know *exactly* how much, say, $1,500 is. You can divide it, multiply it, add to it. It's solid. *"About $1,500"* is more difficult to calculate. How much is *"about $1,500?"*

What if you wanted to know because you were considering buying a business that generates *"about $1,500 a day?"*

To make your decision, you multiply $1,500 per day by 30 days – $45,000 per month. You multiply that by 12 months. Can you count on $547,500 per year? That's a half-million dollar-a-year decision. Can you rely on "*about* $1,500 a day" or should you know exactly?

What if you bought the business, it earned $450,000, and you went bankrupt? Someone might say, "That's *almost* half-a-million dollars. How could you go bankrupt?"

You might say, " I was *only* $97,500 short." Someone else says, "Wow, that's *almost* a hundred thousand bucks." The person that sold you the business says, "That's $1,232.87 a day–*about* $1,500." You say, "I needed *at least* $1,500."

Who would you blame? "*About*" cannot be accurately calculated. **Keep "*about*" out of your goal calculation. Be specific!**

If your goal is to buy a car, be specific. Know the make, model, style and color. If money was no object, and the salesperson asked, "How do you want your car equipped?", would you say, "I'll just take whatever you have?" If the car was free, how many options would you decline?

If your goal is to own a *specific* car, and you want the help of your subconscious, then give your subconscious the *details* it needs to order the car. Otherwise, it may deliver the wrong car.

A friend once told me of his boyhood dream to go to sea. His dream began after sailing with his father on a friend's yacht. He described standing on the bow with the sea spray in his nostrils, thinking: "This is how I want to live."

He recalled that same feeling several years later. As he rethought his dream, he realized he had not been specific enough when setting his goal. He left out a major detail. He was stuck on a battleship headed for war.

This same friend's sister always played with money. She loved money. She became a bank teller. Your subconscious gives you what it believes you want.

Be *specific*. Write your goal on a piece of paper. If it's a money goal, are there dollars and cents signs? If your goal is something physical, can you see it? If so, take a picture of it. Put the picture somewhere you will see it. When you look at the picture ask yourself,

> *"How can I get it? What can I do right now,*
> *this minute, to get it?"*

Build a "fire of desire" for it. Stay focused on it. Convince your subconscious that you must have it. You'll get it.

It's easy.

If I was asked to name the most positive person I've ever known, Bill Wyland and his brother Wyland (no first name) would both be on my short list.

Wyland has distinguished himself as the "world's greatest ocean artist." He understands goal-setting.

He set a 30-year goal to paint 100 life-size "whaling walls" throughout the world. That's specific! It's also an enormous project. So far he's painted 67 walls. He has 33 more walls to paint in the remaining 12 years. He's right on track to meeting his target. His goal is **"The Boss."**

His goal is *specific*. He knows he can do it. He did not know he would also become rich and famous. That wasn't his goal – it was a bonus.

Your goal should be **reasonable**. You must be able to imagine success. *A goal deemed unreachable is nonexistent.*

At the time you establish your goal, your subconscious has an immediate reaction. If that reaction is "No way, forget it," it's all over.

On the other hand, the goal should not be *too easy*.

 Set goals that make you grow and achieve. Your ideal goal is a stretch, but possible.

To be sure if your goal is *reasonable*, compare it to past performances.

When Olympic athletes compete, they have one or more of four specific numbers burning in their brain.

Personal record.

National record.

Olympic record.

World record.

They all have the "fire of desire." Some set goals to break personal records, others to break the world's record. What is believable is conceivable.

Make sure your goal is specific and reasonable, then make it **visible.**

Looking at a picture of your goal creates a "thought trigger." The more you think about your goal, the more dominant it becomes. Once your goal becomes your dominant thought, your subconscious targets it, and "bingo!" you're over the bar enjoying the "whistles and fish."

It's easy.

Bill Wyland is the brother of famed environmental artist Wyland. Together they've built the largest chain of fine art galleries in Hawaii.

In five years they expanded from one "country art gallery" to 16 fine art galleries and $20 million a year in sales.

Bill Wyland is probably *the* most positive person I know. I knew Bill during his first five years of dramatic success.

He progressed from living in a little beach shack to a multi-million-dollar estate high on a hill overlooking Oahu's North Shore.

At the same time, he has created job opportunities for hundreds of people in Hawaii to enjoy success.

This was all done during a very difficult economic period. Hawaii suffered from a depressed economy. The Gulf War caused major decreases in tourism. Retail businesses lowered their advertising budgets, trimmed their staffs and closed marginal locations.

I was eating breakfast with Bill Wyland when the waitress placed a newspaper on the table. The headline said: "Tourism at its lowest point in 50 years."

Bill looked at the headline and said, "I sure hope these tough times continue for a while longer. Look what's happening: art gallery owners are giving up and I'm getting their good locations."

He identified several recent galleries he had acquired and added, "We're doing great. We're setting records every month. Can you imagine how we'll do when the economy is good? I want to get a few more locations before it gets too easy."

At the time, Bill owned a Chevy Blazer. I entered his office, noticed a new picture on his wall and asked, "What is that?" He replied, "That's my new car."

It was a gray-black Mercedes Benz convertible – top of the line.

I asked where it was and he said, "Oh, I haven't bought it yet."

He saw a picture of the car he wanted, cut out the picture, framed it, and hung it in his office.

A few weeks later, Bill guided me out to the parking lot. There sat a shiny new jet black Mitsubishi sports car. He was beaming as he said, "Jump in. I'll take you for a ride."

I asked him about the Mercedes on his wall. "Oh yeah," he said, "I'm still going to get it. But I got such a great deal on this Mitsubishi that I couldn't resist it." Bill loved his new car, yet he didn't take down the picture of the Mercedes.

A few months later he ushered me out to see a jet-black Mercedes Convertible. He explained that it wasn't new, but he got such a good deal he couldn't turn it down.

When he tried to put the convertible top down it wouldn't work. Bill said, "Just a couple of problems – it was in a small wreck, but isn't she a beauty?"

Can you guess what transpired? He kept the picture up on the wall. Two months later, while getting his used Mercedes repaired, he saw it. It was on the showroom floor, a brand-new, gray-black Mercedes just like in the picture on the wall. You guessed it: he bought it.

In Bill's mind he ordered the car the day he hung the picture on the wall. It was delivered when he least expected it.

It was easy. Hang a picture – get a car.

Make your goals as *visible* as you can. Sophisticated business people have back-rooms and offices that look like kindergarten classrooms. They have goals, charts, contests and prizes, all visually displayed in bright colors. They make their goals visual, and keep them in sight.

Do the same thing for yourself. Pick a place that you look at every day. Designate an area in that space to display your goals.

Anytime you need an "attitude adjustment," look at your goals.

 Attitude determines behavior; behavior determines results.

Make your goals *specific, reasonable, visual* and *measurable* so that they attract your subconscious powers.

To remain motivated, track your progress towards your goal.

Companies retain me for one reason – to increase revenue. My first question to the owners is always: "How much revenue are you generating now?" This question usually leads to a display of computer "spread sheets," and long columns of numbers.

Your subconscious responds best to images and feelings. My first suggestion is to display the numbers visually so you can clearly see three things:

1. **THE GOAL** – Where you are going.
2. **THE TRACK** – Where you should be right now.
3. **THE TRAIL** – Where you are right now.

 Any job, task or goal can be broken down into small, manageable parts.

During a marathon, someone stands by the roadside and holds up a sign telling all of the runners how far they have run.

The night before my marathon run, I calculated exactly what my elapsed time should be at these various markers.

I could see the sign, look at my watch, then check my plan. I wrote my plan on a waterproof piece of paper, and put it in my pocket. My plan kept me on target. **It made success easy.**

I learned the need for pacing in earlier, shorter races. You have to block out the urge to race with the thousands of other runners, and follow your own plan.

That's how it is in life. Make your own plan and follow it. Be sure it's *specific* and *reasonable*. Make it *visual* and *measurable*.

It's easy.

Athletes try to dunk the ball into the *basket*, run it into the *end zone*, put it into the *cup*, shoot it into the *pocket*, kick it into the *net* and pitch it into the *strike zone.* They try to hit the ball over the *fence* and out of the *ballpark.*

In football, the playing field is 100 yards long; 10 yards make a first down. Everyone knows how many yards it is to the goal. The "goal post" is *visual,* the yards are *visible* and *measurable.* The clock is running... it's all numbers.

Baseball players know their batting averages. It changes every time they play, but they always know it.

A .300 batting average means three hits for every 10 times at bat.

Batting averages are easily calculated and scrutinized by managers, coaches and opposing pitchers. If baseball players didn't track their batting averages, they might all feel like failures. You see, batting .300 means failing seven times out of 10. But, because it is *measured,* *tracked* and *compared,* they know .300 is good, not bad.

Only the very best hitters average over the .300 mark; .250 is considered average. Hit .200 and you're a "bum." Hit .350 and you're a "superstar." Hit .400? Well... it was last done by Ted Williams of the Boston Red Sox in 1941.

Forty years later, a young ballplayer named George Brett came close. He set his goal to hit .400 and batted .390. He was *reaching for the stars.*

I read a story about a reporter who was watching George Brett take batting practice. The reporter asked casually, "Hi George, how ya doin'?" George replied,

Chapter 7

Scorecards Make Success Easy

"When you face reality and like what you see,
it inspires and motivates you...
When you face reality and don't like what you see,
it inspires and motivates you."

In professional sports everyone watches the scoreboard and the clock. Everyone knows the score and how much time is left to play. The score keeps everyone involved, spectators and participants alike.

To appreciate the motivating force of keeping score, try this. Pick any sport and play it *without* keeping score. How long would you hit a tennis ball back and forth across the net without keeping score?

Imagine 22 men running up and down a football field without knowing who was winning. Imagine 80,000 people watching little stick figures running around the field or court, without a scoreboard.

Whether it's golf, bowling or canasta, you wouldn't play long without a score-sheet of some kind.

Exotic scoreboards are part of professional sports. Sirens wail, fireworks explode and rockets ignite when points are scored.

Are grown men and women with multi-million dollar salaries really motivated by these theatrics? **Yes!**

Is this celebration for the fans, or is it "whistles and fish" for the players? **Yes! Yes!**

The score provides instant feedback. Immediately after the basketball is dunked, two points go on the scoreboard. Fans scream and thrust their arms into the air.

Football running backs cross the goal line, six points go up on the scoreboard and the fireworks explode. The runner was just pummeled by four or five 300-pound musclemen, yet he jumps up and dances in the end zone.

Touchdown celebrations are so elaborate that rules have been enacted to control this display of emotion. Without the clearly defined goal and the six points, no one would take such a beating. No one would feel like dancing. There would be nothing to celebrate.

Only three points are at stake when the field goal kicker comes onto the football field. Many times those three points determine who wins.

Imagine, it's the Super Bowl. The score is 28 to 26. There is only one second left on the clock.

The trailing team has the ball. It's on the 30-yard line. The uprights are standing tall for all to see. A huge, raucous crowd hushes to a silence. The ball is snapped.

This second in life is important for 100,000 people in the stadium. 100,000,000 more are watching on T.V. Everyone is frozen.

What if no one was keeping time and score? How important would that one second out of 3,600 seconds of a football game be?

 Feedback allows you to make minor adjustments. Minor adjustments make success easy.

Feedback creates "thought triggers." When you analyze your performance, you are facing reality.

When you face reality, and like what you see, it will inspire and motivate you.

When you face reality and don't like what you see, it also will inspire and motivate you. So, to be continuously inspired and motivated, continuously face reality.

It's Easy!

 The basic animal reaction when facing danger is to fight it, or run from it. *Fight* or *flight*.

You may have that same animal reaction when you face your performance – reality. ***Fight* or *flight.***

It's been estimated that more than half of all the points scored in football are scored in the last two minutes of each half of the 60-minute game.

What's so different about the last four minutes from the other 56 minutes of the game? The goal changes! The only goal during this last four minutes is to score, and they score.

Players run faster and harder. They throw the ball farther. They take chances they wouldn't ordinarily take. Teams come from behind in the waning seconds because they choose *fight* over *flight.*

You, too, can miraculously come from behind and reach your goals in the final hour. You, too, can choose *fight* over *flight.*

 Face reality, stay motivated. It's easy.

The score is reality. The score is **"The Boss."** Face **"The Boss."** In sports, the scoreboard stays up when your team falls behind. The game continues even when it's obvious who's going to win. **Everyone keeps playing.**

When you fall behind on your goals you could give up. You could stop keeping score. Many people do.

It's your choice, *fight* or *flight.*

Let's say you want to lose weight. If you continue the same behavior, you will keep the same weight.

When you step on the scale, the feedback might be discouraging. You might start telling yourself, "I *can't* lose weight." So, why step on the scale? Who needs the aggravation? Right? **Wrong!**

Fight **or** *flight.*

Let's say you decide to save more money. If you want to save more money, but don't change your financial behavior, you won't save any more money. You'll have a static savings account, or maybe even a dwindling one.

Eventually, you may decide you *can't* save any money. Then you bury your little savings account book in a drawer.

Out of sight, out of mind!

MAKING SUCCESS EASY IS EASY.

*"What I need is someone who will
make me do what I can..."*
RALPH WALDO EMERSON

It sounds like Emerson was asking for a boss. Bosses make people do what they can. Let's say your boss offered to "shadow you" for a full week to help you be your best. Would you improve? Would your behavior be different? Would you feel pressured? Would you try your best? How many things would you do differently?

Would the presence of the boss make you more successful?

Success is Easy

1. **Decide what you want – success can be anything.**
2. **Decide when you want it – have a sense of urgency.**
3. **Make your goal visual – keep it visible.**
4. **Create feedback – know the score.**
5. **Face reality – face the boss – choose *fight* over *flight*.**
6. **Use positive affirmations – sell yourself on success.**

"THE BOSS"

"The Boss" is a visual tool to track your way to success.

Anytime you want to achieve something:

Make it easy – get help from "The Boss."

"The Boss" will make your dreams come true.

"The Boss" will communicate your goals to your subconscious mind.

"The Boss" will make success easy.

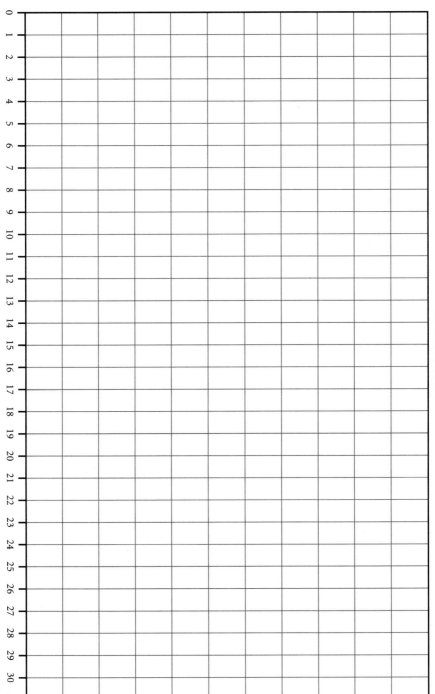

"THE BOSS"

Here are examples of **"The Boss"** at work. You will notice a variety of applications. Everyone's goals are different, and personal.

"The Boss" is also printed on the last pages of this book to make reproduction easy. I grant you permission to copy **"The Boss"**. Enjoy life, and get what you want.

It's easy.

THE END

"The Boss" at work:

Weight Control
Month 1

Losing weight is a popular desire. Joey set a goal to lose 28 pounds total, nine of it in the first month. He asked **"The Boss"** for help. The straight diagonal line represents the *track*. Joey's goal this month is to *trail* the track from his starting weight of 203 pounds to this month's goal of 194 pounds. **"The Boss"** is watching.

Notice how successful **"The Boss"** was, except during Joey's four days of travel. **"The Boss"** stayed home.

The 25th and 26th indicate Joey's overconfidence. Joey got a wake-up call from **"The Boss."** Behavior changed and success was reached on the last day of the month.

To reach his goal Joey must face "The Boss" every day.

1. Step on the scale.
2. Make the dot.
3. Draw the line.

"The Boss" will take care of the rest.
It's easy.

Month 1
Weight Control

"THE BOSS"

Joey
Goal – 194

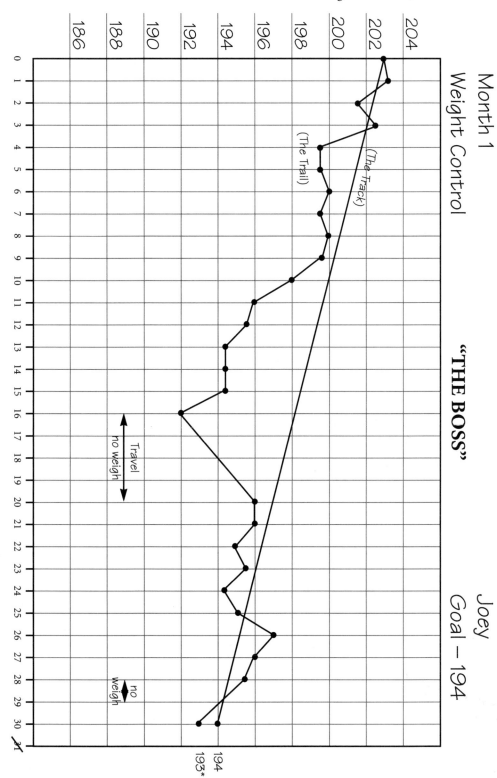

(The Trail)

(The Track)

Travel
no weigh

no
weigh

194
193*

Weight Control
Month 2

Here we see T.I.A.D. (Thumb In Armpit Disease) at work on Joey. Having successfully reached his weight goal in June, Joey's discipline slipped in July.

July 16 was a significant day for Joey. **"The Boss"** said, "*Fight* or *flight.*" Joey considered firing **"The Boss."** Joey chose *fight* over *flight,* kept **"The Boss"** on the job and changed his behavior.

Joey missed his weight goal of 188 this month, but he lost two more pounds.

Next steps: Face reality – face "The Boss."

1. Set a new goal.
2. Make the dots.
3. Draw the lines.

"The Boss" will take care of the rest.
   It's easy.

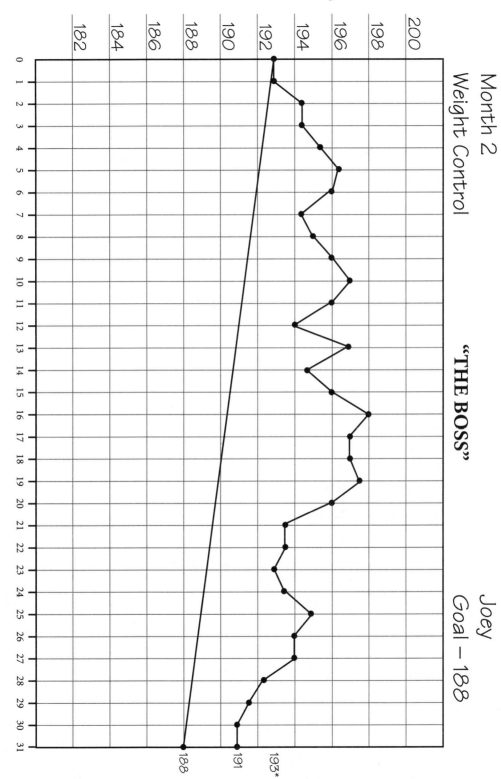

Month 2
Weight Control

"THE BOSS"

Joey
Goal – 188

Weight Control
Month 3

Joey's goal this month was to lose five more pounds and reach 186 pounds by the end of the month. As you can see, choosing *fight* over *flight* paid off.

Joey made the dots and drew the lines. He faced **"The Boss."** By mid-month, Joey's behavior was tied to his results. **"The Boss"** was watching. Joey's behavior changed dramatically, and his weight plummeted to 182 pounds.

Success – Easy.

Next month: Face reality – face "The Boss."

1. Set a new goal.
2. Make the dots.
3. Draw the lines.

"The Boss" will take care of the rest.
It's easy.

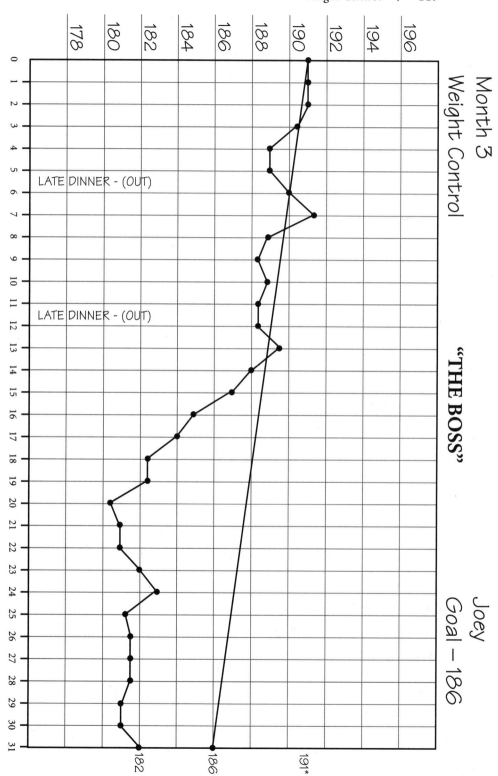

Month 3
Weight Control

"THE BOSS"

Joey
Goal – 186

LATE DINNER - (OUT)

LATE DINNER - (OUT)

Weight Control
Month 4

Joey's goal this month is to lose three pounds and weigh 179. Too easy! He reached his goal by the fourth day of the month. On the 10th day, his weight crept over 179, so he established a new *flat line goal* at 179 and drew it on the chart.

Joey's weight dropped to 175.5 by mid-month, then a late-night celebration caused a big jump on the scale. Joey faced **"The Boss,"** drew a new *flat line* goal at 177 and his weight dropped to 174 by the 19th.

Joey's weight then climbed to 176.5 on the 21st and he established a new *flat line* goal at 175. The original goal of losing 28 pounds was achieved. **"The Boss"** got the job done.

Next month, Joey drew a *flat line* goal at 175.

To maintain your desired weight:
Face reality – face "The Boss" everyday.

1. Step on the scale.
2. Make the dot.
3. Draw the line.

"The Boss" will take care of the rest.
   It's easy.

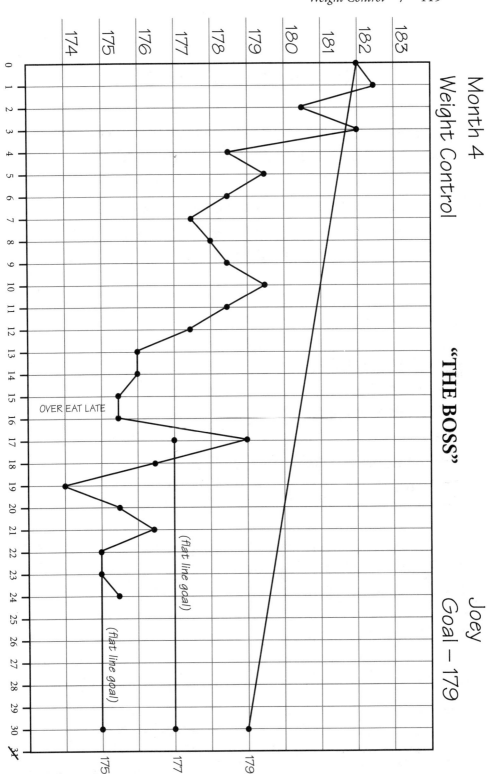

Month 4
Weight Control

"THE BOSS"

Joey
Goal – 179

Savings Account

Suzie's goal is to save $100 next month. **"The Boss"** will help. Suzie made deposits on the 5th, 12th, 19th and 26th of the month.

The *trail* shows Suzie reached and exceeded her goal. She added $130 to her savings account. Next month, Suzie will set a new goal and put **"The Boss"** to work again.

She will: face "The Boss."

1. Make the deposit.
2. Make the dot.
3. Draw the line.

"The Boss" will take care of the rest.
   It's easy.

Month 1
Savings Account

"THE BOSS"

Suzie
Goal – Save $100

$150
135
120
105
90
75
60
45
30
15

DEPOSITS
0 1 2 3 4 5 6 7 8 9 10 11 12 13 14 15 16 17 18 19 20 21 22 23 24 25 26 27 28 29 30 31

$30 $50 $20 $30

$130.00

Retail Sales

This retail store, The Light House, has a goal to have sales of $30,000 next month. Sales *trailed* behind the *track* until the 6th of the month, then climbed above it.

Sales also let up between the 13th and the 16th.

"The Boss" sounded the alarm on the 17th. The store responded and succeeded with $40,000 in sales for the month. **It was easy.**

The Light House will reach and exceed its sales goals; You can too. Face reality – face "The Boss."

1. Calculate your daily sales.
2. Make the dot.
3. Draw the line.

"The Boss" will take care of the rest.

It's easy.

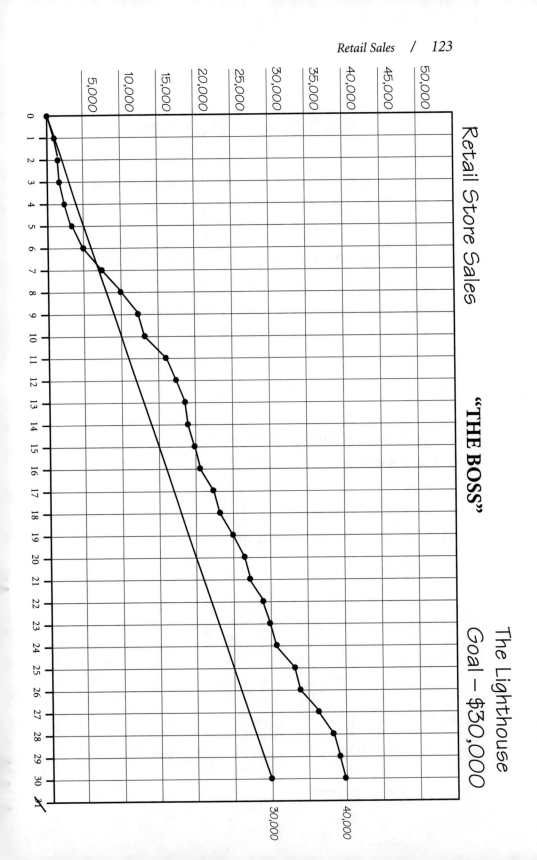

Retail Store Sales

"THE BOSS"

The Lighthouse
Goal – $30,000

Checkbook Balance

This month, Inez wants to increase her average checkbook balance from $550.00 to $800.00.

"The Boss" watched. She did it.

She made a deposit or wrote a check on the 2nd, 7th, 10th, 15th, 18th, 21st, 23rd and 28th. By the end of the month, Inez's checkbook balance was $900.00.

To control your checkbook:
Face reality – face "The Boss."

1. Make deposits and write checks.
2. Make a dot.
3. Draw the line.

"The Boss" will take care of the rest.
   It's easy.

Checkbook Balance

"THE BOSS"

Inez
Goal – $800 Balance

$1,000
900
800
700
600
500
400
300
200
100

0 1 2 3 4 5 6 7 8 9 10 11 12 13 14 15 16 17 18 19 20 21 22 23 24 25 26 27 28 29 30 31

900
800

Mountain Bike Mileage

Pete is a mountain bike enthusiast. He wants to ride 300 miles every month to maintain his physical stamina and condition. He takes **"The Boss"** with him.

This month he rode on the 4th, 7th, 11th, 15th, 19th, 22nd, 25th and 28th.

After his ride on the 25th, **"The Boss"** reminded him that he had 30 miles left and only five days to ride.

Pete faced **"The Boss,"** rode 60 miles on the 28th and surpassed his goal.

To ride 300 miles every month, Pete needs to:
Face reality – face "The Boss."

1. Get on the bike.
2. Make the dot.
3. Draw the line.

"The Boss" will take care of the rest.
　　It's easy.

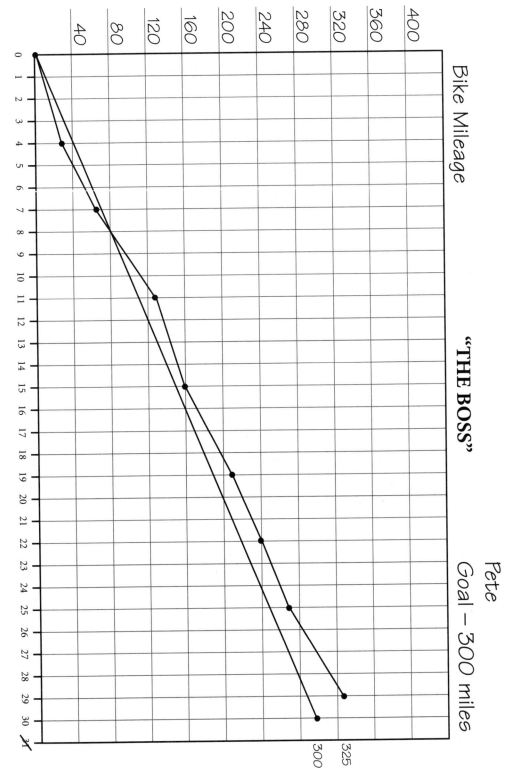

Bike Mileage

"THE BOSS"

Pete
Goal – 300 miles

Walking Time

Hilde wants to walk every day for a total of 25 hours in the month. She takes **"The Boss"** with her.

She *trailed* her *track* until the 14th of the month; then Hilde faced **"The Boss"** and chose *fight* over *flight*. She reached her goal.

To reach her walking goals every month Hilde must: Face reality – face "The Boss."

1. Take a walk.
2. Make the dot.
3. Draw the line.

"The Boss" will take care of the rest.
It's easy.

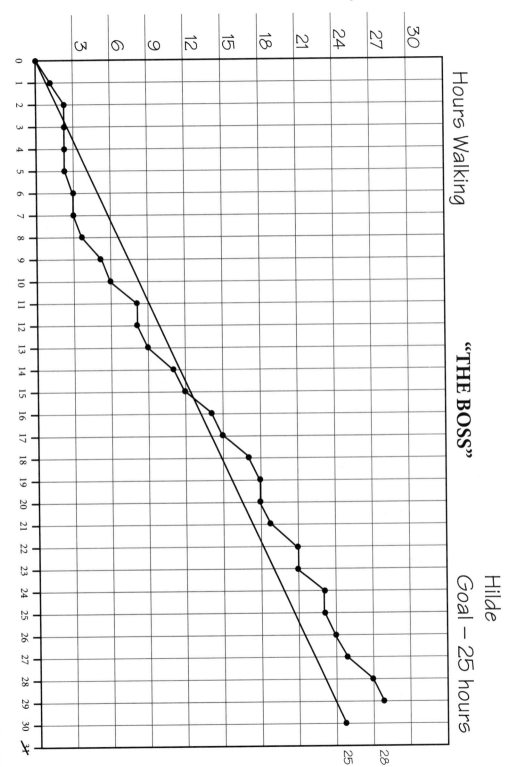

Hours Walking

"THE BOSS"

Hilde

Goal – 25 hours

Exercising

Ron has a busy schedule, but he wants to exercise. He sets goals every month to stretch, do sit-ups and push-ups. **"The Boss"** keeps him motivated.

His goals this month are to stretch for 200 minutes, do 1150 sit-ups and 540 push-ups.

He achieves and raises these goals every month. He keeps **"The Boss"** on the job. He stays in shape.

Put yourself in Ron's shoes on the 19th of the month. Can you feel **"The Boss"** nudging?

You can start exercising right now by getting down on the floor and stretching. Do it again tomorrow. *Track* the time you spend exercising.

Work out with **"The Boss."**

Make it visual. Make it fun. Move more:
Face reality – face "The Boss."

1. Set your goal.
2. Make the dots.
3. Draw the lines.

"The Boss" will take care of the rest.
　　It's easy.

Stretching

"THE BOSS"

Ron
Goal – 200 Minutes

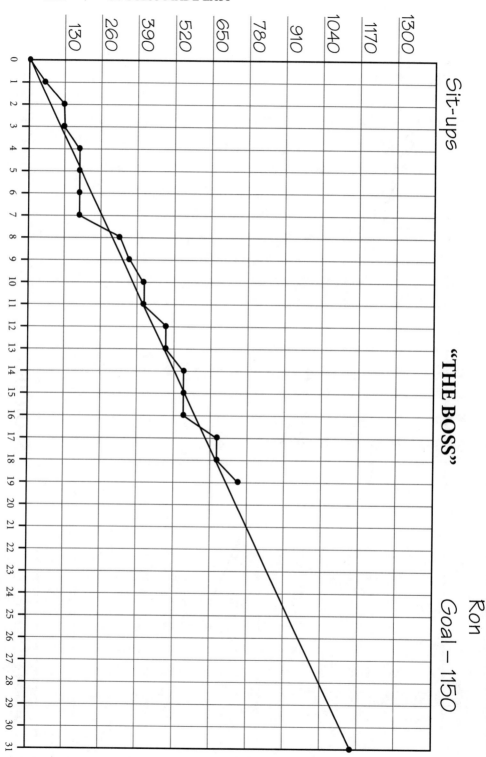

Sit-ups

"THE BOSS"

Ron
Goal – 1150

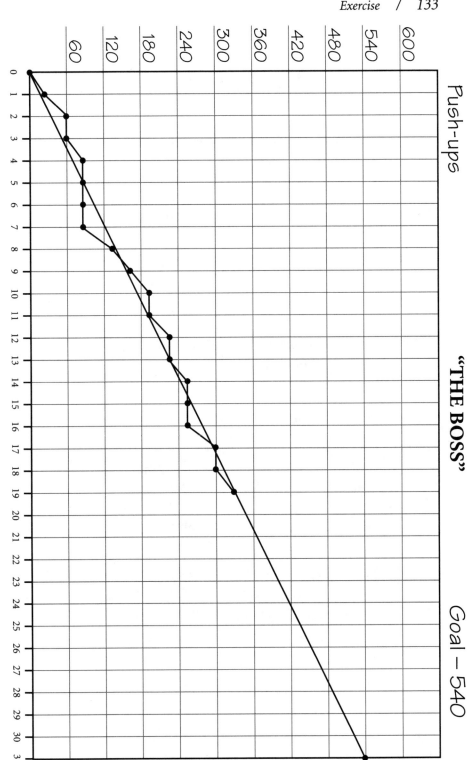

"THE BOSS"

Push-ups

Ron
Goal – 540

Bill Paying

Everyone pays bills. Some people spend time worrying about them. Some forget to pay them.

"The Boss" helps Chris to organize his bill paying. Chris puts a slash mark on the date the bill is due, then X's it off as he pays it.

This frees Chris' mind from worry so he can earn enough money to pay his bills.

"The Boss" will help Chris, but Chris must face reality – face "The Boss."

1. Identify due dates.
2. Make the slash.
3. Make the X.

"The Boss" will take care of the rest.
   It's easy.

Bill Paying

"THE BOSS"

Chris

	0	1	2	3	4	5	6	7	8	9	10	11	12	13	14	15	16	17	18	19	20	21	22	23	24	25	26	27	28	29	30	31
Rent		X																															
Car Ins.				X																													
Cable						X																											
1st Card						X																											
VISA											X																						
1st Deposit												X																					
Car Paymt.													X																				
Phone															X																		
LH																					X												
Paper Boy						X																											
AMEX																																	

House Maintenance

David uses **"The Boss"** to organize his household chores. David schedules an activity with a slash, then crosses it off as he completes it.

Some tasks are more enjoyable than others. **"The Boss"** makes sure none of them are overlooked.

Put **"The Boss"** on this task and you will never forget anything or waste valuable mind time thinking: "I've got to remember to (do anything)."

It's easy; do these three things:

1. Identify the chores.
2. Make the slash.
3. Make the X.

"The Boss" will take care of the rest.
   It's easy.

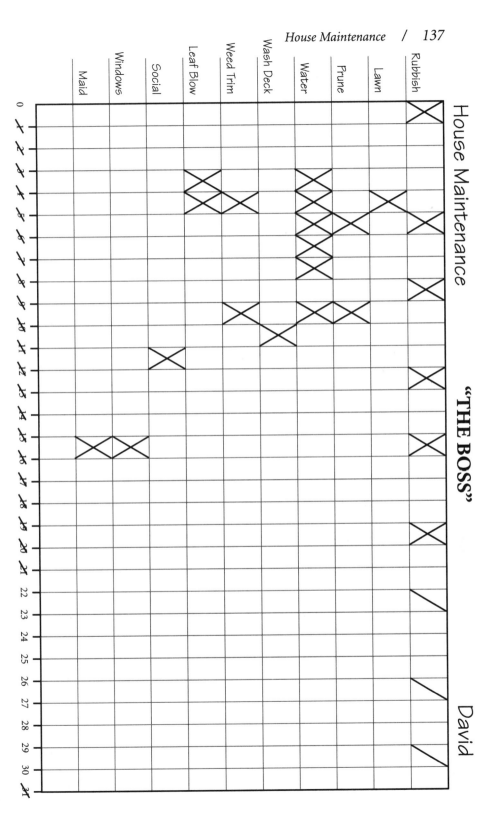

House Maintenance

"THE BOSS"

David

Meditation

Sally set a goal to meditate 20 minutes a day to reach 10 hours for the month. **"The Boss"** kept her on track all month long. Sally never fell behind her goal.

Notice that Sally did not meditate two days in a row, on the 24th and 25th. **"The Boss"** provided a wake-up call and helped Sally reach her goal.

To meditate 10 hours every month, Sally has to:
Face reality – face "The Boss."

1. **Meditate.**
2. **Make the dot.**
3. **Draw the line.**

"The Boss" will take care of Sally.

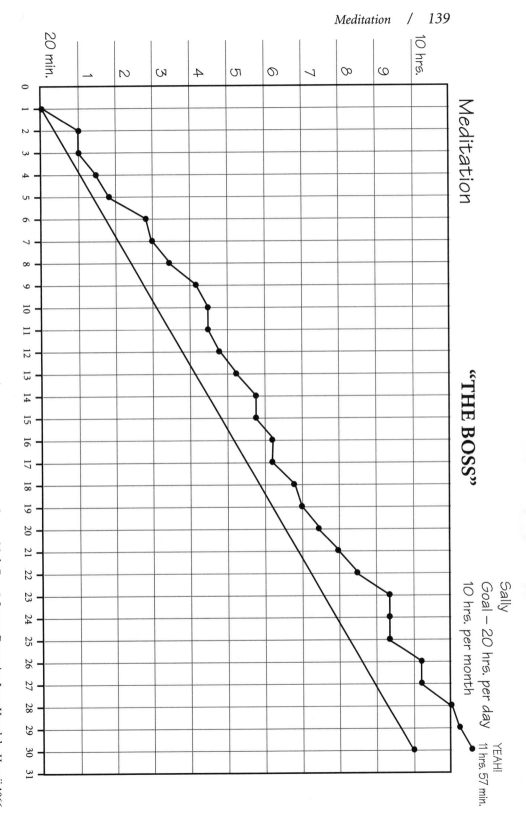

Meditation

"THE BOSS"

Sally
Goal – 20 hrs. per day
10 hrs. per month

YEAH!
11 hrs. 57 min.

Acknowledgements

Many generous people helped me write this book. I thank them all... **they made success easy.**

Mahalo to:

Wyland – For his inspiration. Without his prodding, this book would not exist.

Ruby Pollock – For keying the manuscript, then re-keying it over and over and never complaining.

Michael Fieman – For his constant encouragement and support from the original draft to the last word. Mahalo also for buying the first 100 books.

Rich Budnick – For coaxing and coaching me through the transition from speaker to writer.

Spencer Johnson, M.D. – For teaching me the value and impact of the written word. Also for his straightforward, helpful suggestions and insights that made this a better book by making me a better person.

and to:

Mark Doyle - Becky Ehling - Betty Ling - Ed Randolph - Ed Schneider - Kimberly Van Arsdel
for their editorial advice and assistance.

Doug Behrens - for his graphic genius, personal
professionalism and extreme patience.

Cindy Charlton - for making copy after copy and
always smiling.

Dick Lyday - for transforming the manuscript into
boxes of books.

Mahalo also to the people who willingly read my early thoughts and encouraged me to continue.

Freda Amsel	Kai Farrell	Lloyd Jones
Sandy Arntzen	Gloria Fazendin	Bonnie Jones
Bill Barnfield	Lisa Fazendin	Alexandria Kaaua
Wendy Barnfield	Beverly Fettig	David Kahawaii
Lynn Becker	Ben Fieman	Marty Kahn
Paul Brown	Jason Fieman	Cindy Kama
Nancy Cloud	Therese Gandre	Leslee Kanaiaupuni
Terry Cloud	Jim Geiger	Don Kelly
Karen D'Ascoli	Linda Frutoz Gills	Mary Kelly
Don Dixon	Jo Grande	Steve Kemper
David Dumas	Deborah Greene	"Uncle Billy" Kimi
Corinne Dumas	Lee Hacoen	Cheryl Kojima
Angela Eaton	Maureen Hacoen	Howard Konrad
Marc Eremian	David Hagerman	Ashley Kotomori
Becky Erickson	Diana Hillier	Larry Lee
Pam Farley	Rick Himmelman	Linda Lee
Joyce Farrell	Debbie Hind	Jim Loomis
Mike Farrell	Richard Jacobs	Michael Martin

Fred Martin	Steve Pogni	Cindy Tagavilla
Bob McWilliams	Aness Pogni	Kazumasa Terada
Tao Miller	Alan Pollock	Brick Thompson
Colin Miyabara	John Pyles	Becky Tillery
Bob Moore	Kelly Reed	Tamara Timoshik
Tiffany Murphy	Roy Sakai	Masae Trevino
Cherie Nall	Kathleen Scott	Kent Untermann
Leslie Norton	Dan Schneider	Lori Untermann
Sandi Oguma	Tom Shaw	Ann Watkins
Lorrie Okamura	Yana Shayne	Susan Wels
Robin Peterson	Crawford Sherman	Samantha Wong
Ramona Perkins	Trina Smolen	Bill Wyland
Paki Perkins	Doug Smoyer	Ray Zada
Jeff Pietsch	Terry Snavely	
John Pitre	Jack Stevenson	

and to others who have influenced and added joy to my life. They furthered my ability to write this book.

Caron Abillira	Lazare Hendeles	Art Parent
Honey Girl Abillira	Hal Johnson	Patti Parent
Remi Abillira	Adeline Johnson	Gary Richer
Reno Abillira	Jay Johnstone	Alan Robinson
Zena Abillira	Joey Kammer	Terrie Smith
C.J. Bell	Mike Kammer	W. Clement Stone
Darlene Calvin	Suzie Kauina	Ed Sultan
Larry Carlton	Charlie Lico	Hilde Teijeiro
Margie Chiarello	Linda Martin	David Teijeiro
Madilean Coen	Michelle McGuiness	Bill Welsh
Judy Fenstermaker	Jim McGuiness	
Lindy Flesher	Susan Miles	
Jim Fregosi	Laura Nickliborc	
Lisa Ge	Tom O'Gwynn	
Leilani Gilfoy	Teresa Olsen	
Ross Gilfoy	Peter Ottaviani	
Fred Hendeles	Dorothy Ottaviani	

Ordering Information

You may order additional copies of
"Success Made Easy" from:

Success Dynamics, Inc.
P.O. Box 489
Haleiwa, HI 96712

Phone: (808) 637-5020
Fax: (808) 637-4914
e-mail: easy@aloha.net

Write, call, fax or e-mail us to request current
price list or more information about these books:

"Success Made Easy" by Ron Martin

"Retail Selling Made Easy" by Ron Martin

"Sales Management Made Easy" by Ron Martin

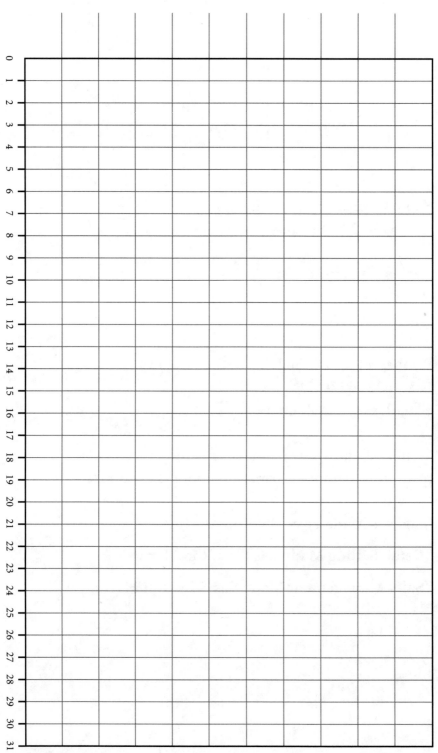

"THE BOSS"

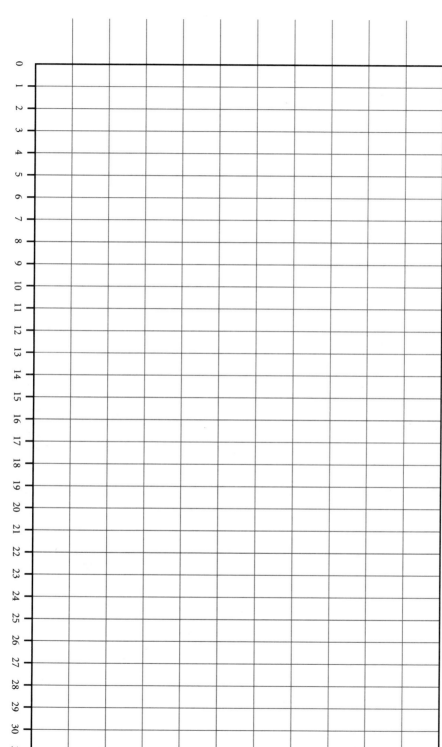

"THE BOSS"

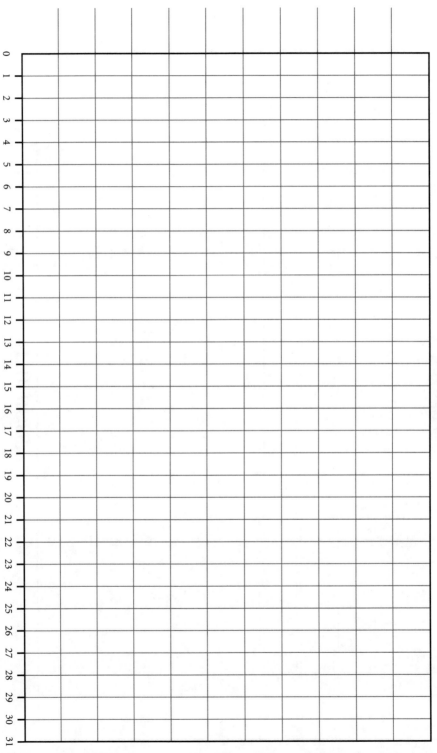

"THE BOSS"

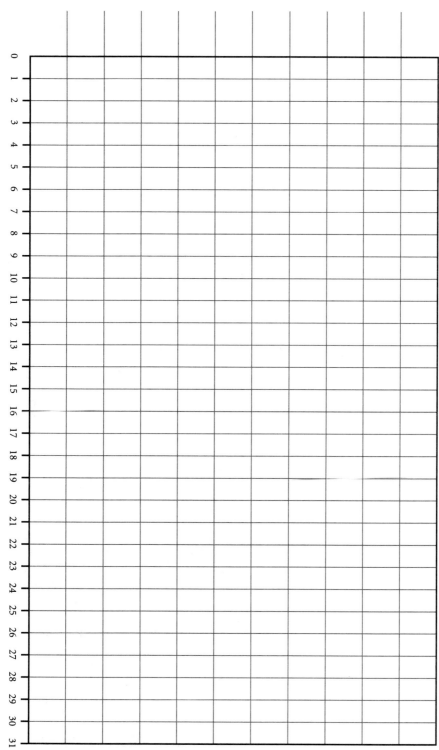

"THE BOSS"

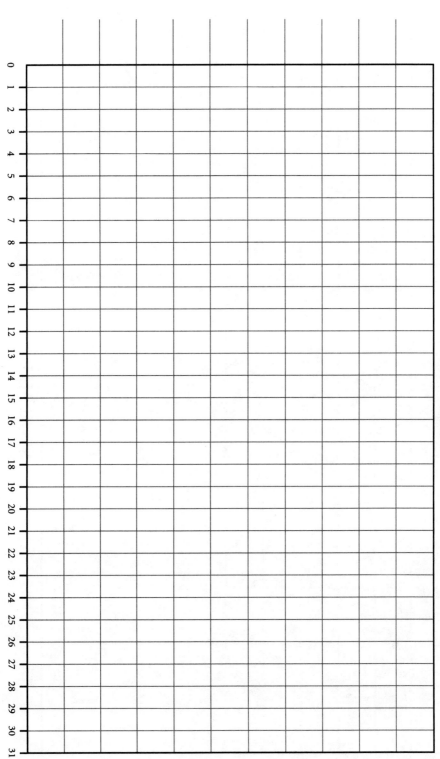

"THE BOSS"